Love _[signature]_

GW00497717

Young**Writers**

WEST YORKSHIRE VOL II

Edited by Allison Dowse

First published in Great Britain in 2003 by
YOUNG WRITERS
Remus House,
Coltsfoot Drive,
Peterborough, PE2 9JX
Telephone (01733) 890066

SB ISBN 1 84460 222 2

FOREWORD

Young Writers was established in 1991 as a foundation for promoting the reading and writing of poetry amongst children and young adults. Today it continues this quest and proceeds to nurture and guide the writing talents of today's youth.

From this year's competition Young Writers is proud to present a showcase of the best poetic talent from across the UK. Each hand-picked poem has been carefully chosen from over 66,000 'Hullabaloo!' entries to be published in this, our eleventh primary school series.

This year in particular we have been wholeheartedly impressed with the quality of entries received. The thought, effort, imagination and hard work put into each poem impressed us all and once again the task of editing was a difficult but enjoyable experience.

We hope you are as pleased as we are with the final selection and that you and your family will continue to be entertained with *Hullabaloo! West Yorkshire Vol II* for many years to come.

CONTENTS

Alissa Smith	48
Robert Coles	49
Emily Durie	49
Joseph Littlewood	49
Lucas Garg-Herrero	50

Roberttown JI CE (C) School

Tom Hague	50
Georgia Trevitt	51
Jack Baldwin	51
Melissa Wallis	52
Emma Bolt	52
Joshua Glassett	53
Ellen-Alyssa Gambles	53
Ellen Bellfield	54
Samuel Bull	54
Kerry Busby	54
David Hall	55
James Ross	55
Hannah Pickering	56
Charlotte Glaves	57
Samuel Crossley	58
Gavin Harrison	58
Kellie-Jo Jeffery	59
Luke Hardy	59
Bethany Stead	60
Alexandra Auty	60
Kirsty Crowther	61
Matthew Stone	61
Kirsty Gee	62
Laylaa Whittaker	62
Georgina Barry	63
Joanna Clarkson	63
Robert Ives	64
Matthew Miller	64
Daniel Mott	65
Laura Baldwin	65
Sara-Jayne Pollard	66

James Booth	67
Bethany Ruston	68
Elliot Binns	68
Abigail Binns	69
Matthew Sumner	69
Hannah Mather	70
Amy Peacock	71
Olivia Jeffery	72
George Edmond	73
Lexy Clavin	74
Bethany Robinson	74
Christopher Thomas	75
Jessica Mott	75
Jacob Sheriff	76
James Sutcliffe	76
Simon Gray	77
Robinson Wade	77
Aimie Crodden	78
Alasdair Hurst	79
Abigail Wallis	80
Thomas Dixon	80
Kate-Arline Miller	81
Siobhan Brogden	81
Shelby Hutchison	82
Natasha Riches	82
Maria Nawaz	83
Richard Brown	83
Alastair McDonald	84
Kerry Brooks	85

St Joseph's RC Primary School, Huddersfield

Martin Tucker	85
Rachel Lamont	86
Kayleigh Paxman	86
Jessica Finn	87
Shauni Macken	87
Sophie Detraux	88
Shannon Fleming	88

Jason Batters	89
Jolene Wike	89
Bret Barraclough	89
Antonia Casson	90
Lucy Calvert	90
Jacob John	91
Shaun Finn	91
Stephen Gandy	92
Lauren Breslin	92
Tanya Allert	93
Charlotte Cosgrove	93
Candice Slee	94
Ben Wilson	94
Oliver Thompson	94
Amber McNulty	95
Joseph Gillespie	95
Shona Peel	96
Joshua Whittaker	96
Jacqueline Wike	97
Joshua McDermott	97
Siobhan O'Toole	98
Luke Chadwick	99
Gillian Harris	99

Seacroft Grange Primary School

Jodie Turnbull	99
Robert Hodgson	100
Mayte Carrington	100
Nathan Hall	100
Tamara Atieno	101
Abeygayle Spink	101
Bethany Dickinson	101
Jason Iddison	102
Matthew Haigh	102
Gemma Matthews	103
Jonathan Turpin	103
Dominic Lynch	104
Demi-Jo Monica Powell	105

The Poems

I LOVE WINTER

I love winter
Sparkling icicles twinkle
in the moonlight.
Families playing,
having fun in the snow.
Your breath-making smoke
in the cold air.
Feel the soft snow
under your shoes.
Building snowmen
slipping and sliding.
Laying in the snow
making snow angels.
Watching the snowflakes
their different shapes
dancing in front of my eyes.
I love winter.

Alistair Wain (8)
Almondbury Junior School

THE CLAW CAT

At night the claw cat strikes
as fast as lightning,
and its fur as soft as white snow.
His eyes
as dark as midnight.
Its voice like hissing of
a mad snake.
His fur as fluffy
as a pillow.

Jamahl Hunte (9)
Almondbury Junior School

AUTUMN IN THE WOODS

Autumn is here, red, brown and gold
leaves falling from the trees,
conkers falling smoothly down whistling songs.
Bushes rustling in the wind,
the wind is whispering,
winter's coming very soon.

I hear the crunching of the leaves
sweet and cool the fragrant air.
I see a hedgehog curling up ready for
its winter's nap,
rustling trees, it's about to rain.
Winter's just a day away.

Marianne Matusz (9)
Almondbury Junior School

WINTER DAYS

Building snowmen over there,
I throw snowballs at their hair!
The ice-cold wind gives me a chill,
The cat sits on the window sill.

The icicles make no sound,
I bet they're worth a million pound!
The ice has started to melt.
I knew how it must have felt.

As the parents start to cheer,
Some start boozing on the beer!
Then the sun starts to appear,
The ice begins to disappear!

Ashley Willcocks (9)
Almondbury Junior School

Winter Is Here

Sledging down the hill I go,
Icicles form very slow.
Snow falls down from the sky,
Ice is thick, I wonder why?

I make a snowman, it takes so long,
I wish the birds were singing a song.
The wind shivers, my toes and hands
I listen to the winter bands.

Is the snowman starting to melt?
Are Scottish people wearing a kilt?
The snowflakes are gone,
There isn't even one.

Dina Lewis (9)
Almondbury Junior School

Cats

Cats are nice,
cats are lovely,
cats are good.

Cat's fur is smooth and silky,
cats catch mice,
cats purr in the night.

Cats keep you warm,
cats go round and round your legs,
cats have different patterns on them,
cats have really sharp claws.

Amy Jade Roberts (9)
Almondbury Junior School

SEASONS

New bloomed flowers swaying in the breeze,
leaves blow softly on the trees.
Newborn lambs struggle to walk,
I wonder if the *baaing* is the only way they talk?

In summer, children are lethargic,
the sparkle in their eyes is magic.
Now I'm starting to get hot and bothered,
Above my head an old bird hovered.

A big star leaf about to flutter,
Crunch, crunch the leaves mutter.
The light colours are orange and yellow,
Not too dark, a kind of mellow.

Winter is bitterly cold,
That's what I'm told.
Though it's not that cold when I'm having fun,
But I still think I prefer the sun!

Shauna Madden (8)
Almondbury Junior School

THE WINTER DREAM

Snowflakes fall to the ground,
people sledging all around,
it starts to snow again,
everyone is having fun,
icicles melting one by one,
snowballs whizzing by,
sun is shining in the sky,
fingers are cold, nose is red,
it is time for home and a warm bed.

Tom Boothroyd (7)
Almondbury Junior School

WHAT IS SHARP?

The blade of an axe.
A drawing pin.
The point of a thorn.
A nettle's sting.

A barber's razor.
A witch's grin.
The stubble
on a giant's chin.

Broken glass.
A rusty nail.
The fangs of a snake.
A scorpion's tail.

Molly Jones & Fern Priestley (8)
Almondbury Junior School

SPELLS

Fat from a pig
Claws to dig
Trunk from an elephant
Legs from an ant
Fingers from the dead
Add some poison lead
A bit of cats' fur
And start to stir
As black as night
Gives you a fright
So you better watch out.

Philip Dimmer (10)
Almondbury Junior School

MICE

I think mice
Are rather nice.
They squeak and squeal
When they search for their meal.

They're small and cute
They like to loot.
A piece of cheese,
Is sure to please.

Watch for the trap . . .
Snap!

Jessica Thornton (9)
Almondbury Junior School

MY CANDLE

My candle flickers in the night,
Making shadows with the light,
I see a circle dancing by,
A triangle touching the sky,
It didn't even have to try.

Anita Pearson (11)
Almondbury Junior School

WINTER DAYS

Winter days are very cold,
Especially when the days grow old.
When the winter days grow older,
The winter days will grow colder.

As the winter draws to end,
It's as though we depend,
On the sun to come out,
Instead of staying in and pout.

Rebecca Shaw (9)
Almondbury Junior School

AUTUMN DAYS

Autumn days, windy nights,
Brown leaves falling down.
Hedgehogs curling as night goes by.

The wind whistling in the night.
In the day, bye, bye, birds.
Mums and dads, feel the cold.

Crisp and cool through the night
Winter's on its way.
Scaring us away.

James Taylor (9)
Almondbury Junior School

OLD AGE

Old age is painful.
It smells like out of date bananas.
Old age tastes sickly and bitter.
It sounds like breaking bones,
It feels damp and sharp.
Old age lives in the heart of wrinkles!

Kerr Jagger (9)
Almondbury Junior School

HIDDEN BEAUTY

The moonlight flower dwells,
Behind the crooked trees,
No sunshine shines around it,
Just moonlight that it sees.

The moonlight flower blinds,
From the hidden beauty of its bloom,
It sprinkles clouds of pollen,
That smells like sweet perfume.

The moonlight flower silver and blue,
Dances in the breeze,
Yet nothing knows of its existence,
As it hides behind the trees.

The moonlight flower in the dark,
Shines with all its might,
It's a flower of secrecy
And has no need of light.

The moonlight flower dwells,
Behind the crooked trees,
No sunshine shines around it,
Just moonlight that it sees.

Emma Kilroy (11)
Almondbury Junior School

WINTER TIMES

A shower of ice-cold snow is forming,
I get up early whilst it's dawning.
The ice is slippery and very hard,
I cheer up my friend with a Christmas card.

I shiver through the ice and snow,
And slip and fall and say, 'Ouch oh.'
Me and my friend have a snowball fight,
Whilst the earth is black and white.

Gregory Selbie (8)
Almondbury Junior School

CATS

Toby was a big black cat,
He was round and furry and very fat.
He slept all day and went out at night,
Chasing little mice and starting a fight.

Scaring and scratching the poor little mice,
Toby really wasn't very nice.
The frightened mice hatched a plan,
To get rid of Toby any way they can.

They hired a dog who was big and scary,
He had sharp fierce teeth and was black and hairy.
One day when Toby went out to play,
He saw the dog growling and barking away.

The dog stared at Toby and showed his big teeth,
Toby ran to a car and crawled underneath.
He didn't come out until he saw the dog go,
How could Toby say he was sorry, he wanted to know?

He gave the mice a nice piece of cheese,
With a note saying 'I'm sorry, be my friend please.'
The mice forgave Toby and became his friend,
They all played happy together.
The End.

Chelsea Leigh Hinchliffe (7)
Almondbury Junior School

Isn't My Name Magical?

Nobody can see my name
My name is inside
And all over me, unseen,
Like other people also keep it.
Isn't my name magic?
My name is only mine
It tells I am individual.
The one special person it shakes
When I am wanted.
If I'm with hundreds of people
And my name is called,
My sound switches me on to answer
Like it was my human electricity
Isn't it magical?
My name echoes across the playground,
It comes, it demands my attention,
I have to find out who calls,
Who wants me for what?
My name gets blurted out in class,
It is a terror at a bad time,
Because somebody is cross,
My name gets called in a whisper
I am happy because
My name may have touched me
With a loving voice.
Isn't it all magical?

Rachita Puri (10)
Almondbury Junior School

WINTER AND SNOW

In winter the roads are covered in slushy snow,
All the cars going extremely slow.
I see a snowball fight in the bright shiny light,
Everyone yelling *'Fight, fight, fight!'*

The yard frozen like an icy ring,
Why aren't the birds singing?
All the trees big and bare,
Spring quite nearly there.

The winter is very cold,
Do you think the snow will hold?
Ice on the yard,
Getting extremely hard.

Snowflakes sparkling on the soft ground,
Look everybody what I've found.
The yard covered in cold and gleamy snow,
Spring is coming, extremely slow.

Akash Bhalla (9)
Almondbury Junior School

AUTUMN DAYS

The autumn days have just begun,
All the children are having fun.
All the leaves are brown and gold,
All the trees are very bold.

The autumn winds are blowing hard,
All the trees look very weird.
All the people are dressed very snug,
And there's lots of things like slugs and bugs.

Luke Modeste (8)
Almondbury Junior School

11

MUSIC IS MY LIFE

Music is the best thing that could ever happen to me.
Whenever I listen to it I can feel my soul being set free.

There's rock, pop and even hip hop,
there's top ten and top twenty,
but for me just plain music is plenty.

My mum likes all the classical stuff,
and when we don't want to listen to it she gets all tough.

Dad loves his metal music and when it's on it's on.
In fact it's quite scary when he sings along.

My brother is really not bothered as long as it is not near him.
He's too busy on the computer, isn't he rather dim?

I'm not bothered about what music I listen to because music is
                                                    my life.
When it is taken away from me, it's like being stabbed with a
                                                    knife.

Because music is my life.

Faye Myring (8)
Almondbury Junior School

HUNGER

Hunger is dark and gloomy,
It smells old and rotten,
Hunger tastes like old fruit,
People crying in the alleys,
Feeling tatty and worn,
They live in the darkest alleys.

Adam Senior (10)
Almondbury Junior School

WINTER'S BACK

Winter's coming, wrap up warm,
Because Mr Frost is here.
Trees are thick with a sparkling quilt of snow,
Because winter's here once more.

Look on Christmas Eve,
See the snow lay its sparkling quilt.
Go to bed, sleep, sleep, because Santa's coming.

Rush, rush in the morning.
Run downstairs and open your presents.
See your eyes sparkle with joy
Because winter's back.

In the morning wrap up warm
Making angels in the snow.
All the things that make me shiver are snowflakes,
Wind, rain and the snowflakes dropping.

Cold and shivering slippery ice
All over the cold and gloomy floor.
Cold misty you're so cold because winter's back forever.

Lauren Pascall (8)
Almondbury Junior School

HAPPINESS

Happiness is yellow
It smells like roses
It tastes like fresh spring water
It sounds like families
It feels like friendship
Happiness lives within us.

Calum Wood (9)
Almondbury Junior School

MY CAT

My cat Barney
is very barmy
he sleeps in a bin
he hates to win
he eats bread and butter
without causing a flutter
he reads upside down
he acts like a clown
he's my cat
that sleeps on a mat
while watching telly
he isn't very smelly
he has eight lives
and also has ten wives!
When he dies
there will be lots of cries.
My cat Barney
is very barmy.

Amy Seddon (11)
Almondbury Junior School

STARS

Floating stars in the sky,
don't go I haven't said bye.

Where is the baby?
Or has he gone up to Heaven where he belongs?

Tell me, tell me!
Floating star will I die as well when I go that far?

Chelsea Davies (8)
Almondbury Junior School

BUGS

Spiders, spiders and even more spiders making a web today.
Caught a fly, caught a fly, for my tea, caught a fly,
Caught a fly just for me.

'Centipede, centipede how many legs do you have?'
'One million I suppose I guess that's *me!*'

'Ladybird, ladybird come back again
With your beautiful spots and your babies too.'

'Caterpillar how much leaves do you eat?'
'Five a day if you please.'

Slugs, slugs, ugly slugs,
Really ugly slugs and slimy too.

Alex Roffey (8)
Almondbury Junior School

MY MUM

My mum is lovely with dark brown hair
She taught me how to play and share.

She's got big blue eyes and lips that are red,
She even tucks me tightly into bed.

Her body's all comfy and cuddly and warm
She won't let me come to no harm.

She cuddles me tightly and kisses my nose
She loves me right from my head to my toes.

Her skin is so soft and she smells so nice
My mum is the biggest part of my life.

Emily-Jo Wilkins (10)
Almondbury Junior School

Winter

All the trees are covered in snow
The leaves are falling very low
Sometimes I feel cold and try to keep hold.

Snow is glazing very white.
Glitter falling in the light.

The water in the pond has become frozen ice.
The view from my window is very nice.
I look here, I look there,
Snowflakes falling everywhere.

Arifa Munir (9)
Almondbury Junior School

If I Were A Shape

If I were a shape
I'd be a sphere
I'd be a snooker ball potted by Jimmy White.
I'd be a boulder blocking Ali Baba's cave.
I'd be a football smashed into the back of the net
                        by Ruud van Nistelrooy
If I were a sphere.

If I were a shape
I'd b e a cube
I'd be Santa's house
I'd be a parcel going to lots of different places.
I'd be a box of sweets opening and closing all the time.
If I were a shape.

Joseph Gaskell (11)
Carlton J & I School

IF I WERE A SHAPE

If I were a shape
I'd be a sphere,
I'd be an orange sat alone in the lonely fruit bowl,
I'd be a football rolling across the long grass and shooting
into the back of the net.
I'd be a snowball flying through the cold ice air,
If I were a sphere.
If I were a shape,
I'd be a cube,
I'd be a box stuck in a dusty cupboard,
I'd be an ice cube melting away in the boiling hot sun,
I'd be a blue block of chalk getting ready to be used by a
famous snooker player,
I'd be a dotted dice rolling across the flat games board,
If I were a cube.
If I were a shape,
I'd be a cone,
I'd be a red party hat on someone's hairy head,
I'd be a traffic cone stopping all of the busy traffic,
I'd be a pyramid standing still in the hot sand,
I'd be an ice cream cone cooling the children down,
If I were a cone.

Amy Nutter (10)
Carlton J & I School

MY BROTHER

Moans and groans
Chuckles and giggles
Tickles and laughs and he plays on my bike,
And he hits me and hurts me.
That's my big brother!

Samantha Shaw (9)
Carlton J & I School

IF I WERE A SHAPE

If I were a shape
I'd be a sphere,
I'd be a football with the famous footballer Rio Ferdinand's
signature on it,
I'd be a dusty green planet with no sign of a living thing on it at all,
I'd be a large bumpy boulder on the sunny, warm, sandy beach
on a summer's day,
If I were a sphere.

If I were a shape
I'd be a rectangle,
I'd be a football pitch where Manchester United would always win,
I'd be a five foot chocolate bar which never went mouldy.
I'd be a book you'd read all the time,
If I were a rectangle.

If I were a shape
I'd be a cylinder,
I'd be a can of shandy fizzing you off to space,
I'd be a smelly cigarette puffing smoke all around,
I'd be a cheese and bacon casserole steaming on the plate,
If I were a cylinder.

Rebecca Poole (11)
Carlton J & I School

IF I WAS A SHAPE

If I was a shape I'd be a circle
I'd be a ball getting kicked across the football pitch
I'd be a clock going *tick-tock*
I'd be a bottle lid rolling down the road
If I was a circle . . .

Rachel Black (10)
Carlton J & I School

IF I WERE A SHAPE

If I were a shape
I'd be a cylinder
I'd be a can of Coke fizzing up
Ready to explode while being stacked in a supermarket,
I'd be a pipe stuck underground letting water run through me
                                              until I rusted away,
I'd be a tin of beans opened and left in the corner of the cupboard
                                                        to go off,
If I were a shape.

I were a shape,
I'd be a sphere
I'd be a football going into the back of the net from the right foot
                                              of David Beckham,
I'd be a tennis ball hitting the netting from a faulty serve,
I'd be a cricket ball hitting the wickets from a perfect shot,
If I were a shape.

If I were a shape
I'd be a rectangle
I'd be a football pitch when Liverpool are losing to Man Utd,
I'd be a chocolate bar that had been left to go off and melt,
I'd be a sheet of paper ready for Roald Dahl to use,
If I were a rectangle.

Toby Bailey (10)
Carlton J & I School

IF I WAS A SHAPE

If I was a shape I'd be a round sign, warning people.
I'd be a traffic light changing and blinking.
I'd be a smoke alarm saying 'Fire, fire!'
If I was a circle.

Jack Eastwood (11)
Carlton J & I School

If I Were A Shape

If I were a shape
I'd be a sphere
If I were a shape
I'd be a golf ball lurking at the bottom of a duck pond,
I'd be an everlasting gobstopper that someone has been chewing
for ages,
I'd be a globe turning by an explorer planning on where he
was going next,
If I were a sphere.

If I were a shape
I'd be a cone
I'd be a glittering party hat worn by a diva star,
I'd be a horn of a bull charging at a red sheet,
I'd be a traffic cone holding all the traffic back,
If I were a cone.

If I were a shape
I'd be a cylinder
I'd be a fresh pint of milk off of the milkman on a sunny day,
I'd be a wheel of a steamroller rolling over ready-made tarmac,
I'd be an empty Smartie box thrown in the bin with the rest
of the rubbish,
If I were a cylinder.

Keeley Harvey (11)
Carlton J & I School

If I Were A Shape

If I were a shape,
I'd be a rectangle,
I'd be a classroom light shining on the teacher,
I'd be the biggest book of them all,
I'd be a bar of chocolate with rich hazelnut,
If I were a shape.

If I were a shape
I'd be a sphere
I'd be a golf ball for Tiger Woods,
I'd be a sun at the centre of the solar system,
I'd be an everlasting gobstopper in a child's pocket,
If I were a sphere.

Sean Davis (11)
Carlton J & I School

IF I WERE A SHAPE

If I were a shape
I'd be a cylinder
I'd be a can of Coke flat and forgotten in the corner of the cupboard,
I'd be a steamroller pressing rapidly on the scolding tarmac,
I'd be a sausage sitting in the sizzling pan,
If I were a shape.

If I were a shape
I'd be a cone
I'd be a traffic cone guiding people safely on their way
I'd be an ancient Egyptian pyramid watching over the ancient
pharaohs' bodies,
I'd be a ice cream cone with all the yummy ice cream melting down
the crispy sides,
If I were a cone.

If I were a shape,
I'd be a cube
I'd be a dice in the casinos of Las Vegas rolling to and fro,
I'd be a Rubric's cube the trickiest one of all,
I'd be an ice cube frozen stiff at the back of the fridge
If I were a cube.

Alex Boughen (10)
Carlton J & I School

IF I WERE A SHAPE

If I were a shape
I'd be a circle
I'd be a big wheel on a 4 x 4 driving through the mud,
I'd be a planet in the solar system all on my own
I'd be a pair of traffic lights changing colour every five minutes
If I were a circle.

If I were a shape
I'd be a rectangle
I'd be a chocolate bar melting in the sun,
I'd be a pencil case laying on the table,
I'd be a sheet of coloured paper being drawn on by an artist,
If I were a rectangle.

If I were a shape
I'd be a triangle
I'd be a pyramid on the hot desert sand
I'd be a piece of triangle chocolate in somebody's mouth,
I'd be a building sign telling everyone the road is being fixed,
If I were a triangle
If I were a shape.

Luke Fairhurst (10)
Carlton J & I School

IF I WERE A SHAPE

If I were a shape
I'd be a rectangle
For people to put toys on me to be a shelf,
For people to sit on me to be a cushion mate,
To be sat on like a banana peeling open to be eaten,
If I were a rectangle.

Rebecca Roberts (11)
Carlton J & I School

IF I WERE A SHAPE

If I were a shape
I'd be a circle
I'd be a tyre on a lambourghini as it zooms down the road,
I'd be a planet hanging in an empty solar system all alone,
I'd be a clock hanging on a wall telling everyone the time
If I were a circle.

If I were a shape
I'd be a cone
I'd be an ice cream cone with ice cream on the top
I'd be a tiger's tooth slicing into his prey,
I'd be a warning cone where there is danger,
If I were a cone.

If I were a shape
I'd be a sphere
I'd be a football zooming down the pitch towards the goal,
I'd be a bouncy ball bouncing into outer space,
I'd be a beach ball stranded in the deep blue sea,
If I were a sphere.

Luke Hollinworth (10)
Carlton J & I School

THE LONELY SCARECROW

It stands there all tiny and baggy
No bones to make it look more lifelike.
No clothes on it at all.
Even those he wears are too ragged to describe.
He just stands and awaits the birds.
Those little birds are the only company he has.
But if only they could talk . . .

Daniel Hugill (9)
Carlton J & I School

IF I WERE A SHAPE

If I were a shape
I'd be a sphere
I'd be someone's eye looking everywhere seeing everything,
I'd be the Earth moving slowly around the universe,
I'd be an orange sat in the sun, sat in the fruit bowl,
If I were a sphere.

If I were a shape
I'd be a cuboid
I'd be a tower in the middle of a really busy city,
I'd be a radio blowing out music,
I'd be a brick building up a big house,
If I were a cuboid.

If I were a shape
I'd be a cube
I'd be dice rolling on a board game to win the match.
I'd be a television shining and sleeping,
I'd be a parcel being delivered to the owner,
If I were a sphere.

Daryl Billings (11)
Carlton J & I School

MY SUPER SISTER

My super sister is defiantly good she always tidies up.
We never have to shout at her once.
She always tries to help me when it is breakfast.
My super sister is so good she's never late for school.
Oh no it's the afternoon with my sister.
Oh yes you've got it, it's World War III
Pillow fighting and banana bombs.

Joshua Mills (9)
Carlton J & I School

IF I WERE A SHAPE

If I were a shape
I'd be a sphere
I'd be a muddy football soaring into the back of the net,
I'd be a large, round moon watching over children peacefully sleeping
I'd be a silk, white snowball flying through the air as fast as lightning,
If I were a sphere.

If I were a shape
I'd be a cone
I'd be a glistening party hat on a joyful person's head,
I'd be an ice cream cone with on top cool, refreshing ice cream,
I'd be a cone in the road blocking angry drivers away,
If I were a cone.

If I were a shape,
I'd be a cube
I'd be an ice cube melting away in somebody's drink,
I'd be a dice on a board game rocking to and fro,
I'd be a box of chocolates melting in a jiffy,
If I were a cube.

Charlotte Quinn (11)
Carlton J & I School

MY BROTHER

My brother smokes and chokes,
Spits and kicks,
and hits me with cans and pans,
pencils and stencils,
and moans and groans,
yawns and eats prawns.
What does your brother do?

Nathan Kirby (9)
Carlton J & I School

I'M A SWAN

Gracefully gliding across the lake,
Swimming through seaweed then on the lake.
Flapping my wings before I fall,
Before they're not there at all.
Having much fun with my friends.
When it is time, hear a chime,
Then it's dinnertime.
Eating leaves seems so strange to me
Wishing and wishing how long can it be
Before I hear a whistle?
Everyone's clapping like the down of a thistle.
Rich and famous is what I wish to be,
Help me, help me, before I sleep,
Drifting away, oh I wish I could stay.

Jasmine Evans (8)
Carlton J & I School

MY DAD

My dad he's big and hairy
Dances like a fairy
His eyes are green, his lips are red
He still sleeps with his ted
With golf club in his hand
He gets mad and his pants expand
Slices the ball into the tee
Oh God please help me
Comes home to tea full of woe
He's my dad, I love him so.

Grant Covell (8)
Carlton J & I School

FOOTBALL

Football is so good because you get covered in mud.
You kick a ball then you fall.
You need a referee that gives you a yellow or a red card.
You win or lose, maybe you draw.
That's when you hear the crowd roar.

Lee Sykes (8)
Carlton J & I School

MY SHOP STOCKS . . .

Mops and pops,
dollies and brollies,
pegs and eggs,
tins and bins,
lollies and trolleys,
new rules and new jewels.
What does your shop stock?

Tyler Ryalls (9)
Carlton J & I School

MY SHOP STOCKS . . .

Cherries and berries,
lollies and dollies,
jars and bars,
books and trucks,
sweets and treats.
What does your shop stock?

Richard Sanderson (8)
Carlton J & I School

WHAT MY SHOP STOCKS

My shop stocks . . .
Girls and boys,
Sure love toys.
Like a ball,
A doll,
A game,
The same.
A dolly,
Called Polly.
Instead of Polly,
How about a lolly?
Wouldn't that just do?

Carly Carbutt (9)
Carlton J & I School

MY BROTHER KYLE

My brother Kyle
Has a big smile.

My brother likes to
Talk and talk and talk.

My brother is good
Some of the time.

We all love
This brother of mine.

Garth Halford (8)
Carlton J & I School

HAMSTERS

Jess the hamster lives in a cage.
She eats hamster food.
She drinks water.
They have tiny paws for feet.
They look nice and warm in their fur.
They can have big homes with steps.
They have tunnels.

Ashleigh Kerry (9)
Cliffe Hill CP School

FISH

Jess the fish jumped in her tank
She had some goldfish food.
Jess has gold scales.
Jess swims all day in and out of her log.
Jess sleeps every night.
Jess plays every morning.

Kyle Manchip (8)
Cliffe Hill CP School

FOOTBALL, FOOTBALL

Football shirts are different colours
Football shorts are comfy like pillows.
Football players have lots of layers,
A goalie is a football player.
A referee is so not fair,
A football is full of air!

Reese Fox (8)
Cliffe Hill CP School

I'M A HAMSTER CUDDLY AND FAT

I'm a hamster cuddly and fat.
My house is warm, blue and yellow.
I eat my food in my bed.
I eat Wheeto's and much more.
My feet look like duck's feet.
My feet are webbed.
I drink out of a bottle.
I can only have water.
I have two flats in my house.
But, the best of all I look like a guinea pig.
I sleep in the morning and wake up at night,
And last but not least when I'm awake,
They let me out in my ball.

Rachelle Wheatley (9)
Cliffe Hill CP School

GEMMA THE GOLDFISH

Gemma the little goldfish was swimming in her fish tank,
Lovely colourful scales and very bright skin,
She jumps, swims all day long,
Through the night and through the day
Gemma the fish is busy swimming about in her big fish tank.
Gemma goes through her tunnel.
She never stops, she never rests.

Katie Houghton (8)
Cliffe Hill CP School

GOOD AND EVIL CANNOT MIX

Fairies' wings are colourful,
Mermaids' tails are green as the grass,
Things that I love, I love, I love
Things that I love.

Dragons live in dark, dark caves,
Snow monsters hide in the snow,
Things that I love, I love, I love
Things that I love.

You better hide
Vampires flying in the night
You better hide
Vampires are going to bite.

Evil magic also moves,
From power crazy wizards,
Evil magic is after you.
It's everywhere that you think.

But good and evil cannot mix,
To the red-horned Devil, and the fairy queen.
So now you know that magic lives,
Beware: you could end up in a fix.

Lucie Ellis (10)
Cliffe Hill CP School

THE BRAIN

Compact in your head
A grey matter of fact
Packed with knowledge
So don't get me cracked.

Robyn-Louise Thompson (9)
Golcar JI & N School

THE EFFECTS OF A PILL

Once I was a doctor,
and I took a little pill,
my head started spinning,
and I got very ill.

The cat went fuzzy,
the bee went buzzy too,
I even tore up my uncle's
best shoe.

I looked upon the ocean,
to see what I could see,
and what I saw was a figure,
that looked just like me.

I went out to see
what I could find,
and what I found was,
the boat had left me behind.

I swam for dear life
as I swam to Forfife,
and I went to my bed,
to sort out my life.
And I slowly, slowly sunk down to the ground.
        Goodbye!

Amy Smith (10)
Golcar JI & N School

DUSTBIN BABY

I was dumped in a dustbin,
It was awful, a big metal tin.
My mum dumped me when I was a baby,
Will she come back? Maybe.

I got a new foster mum, Marion's the name,
I just can't stick her, she's such a pain.
I hope in the future it will all be fine,
I'll get a new Mum better than mine.

Hannah Charlesworth (9)
Golcar JI & N School

FLOWERS

Think of a tree all bare in the snow,
Don't you feel sorry for it in the winter cold?
In the winter, snowdrops fall,
It's like someone's sending a message they shout and call.

Near to the spring tulips call and sing,
Roses chatter and gossip, but they don't think it matters.
Daffodils hail and sing while the bluebells twinkle and ring.

What about summer, go ask Nanna,
She'll tell you a rhyme and take her time,
When you think of flower you sense a great deal of power.

Now the job's done, you think it's all just begun,
You've learnt so much in this past couple of months.

Curl up by the fire, your friend's coming for tea,
She's called Mya,
Have a great time, think of something happy,
Up in your mind.

Come on curl up in your bed, go to sleep,
Sleep head, forty winks for a boy, forty winks for a girl,
Curl up with cuddly toy, it's called Pearl.
        Have a great sleep make it worth
                Your peace.

Yasmin Russell (10)
Golcar JI & N School

WORDS

Words, words, words, everywhere,
Words, words, words, somewhere.
Words on TV, take a look,
You'll see enough in a book.
Words on boards,
Words on drawers,
Words on floors,
And words some more.

Words are crazy,
Others are lazy.
Words are sweet,
And very neat.

Megan Grainger, Natalie Hunt & Georgina Walters (9)
Golcar JI & N School

LAST IN THE QUEUE

When they gave out the toys
I was last in the queue.
There were no bats or play dough.
Lego or Barbies,
Teddies or telescopes,
Balls or bionics,
Action man or doctors,
Bayblades or baby dolls,
Roller blades or scooters,
Skateboards or bikes,
There was only a bouncy castle,
The trouble is I don't have enough room.

Charlotte Staniuszko (8)
Golcar JI & N School

NAMEZ

B to the E to the N
I am back again
Wit my best pen.

J to the A to the C to the K
That spells Jack
I say it every day

T to the O to the M
Ya betta watch out
I'm back again.

'Ben, Ben, where 'ave ya been?'
'Jack, Jack, please come back,'
'Tom, Tom, where 'ave ya gon'?

B to the E to the N
J to the A to the C to the K
T to the O to the M.

We are real men!

Ben Graham, Thomas Handley & Jack Lucas (10)
Golcar JI & N School

HEART

Small and round
Red and blue
Lumpy and bumpy
In the chest
Bump thump bump.

Hannah Gilroy (10)
Golcar JI & N School

Last In The Queue

When they gave out the sweets
I was last in the queue.
There were no jelly babies or coconut sweet.
Chocolate eclairs or Snickers
Bounty or marshmallows.
Double Deckers or bom boms
Liquorice or treats
Fruity chews or nutty M & M's
Dolly Mixtures or Smarties
Kit Kats or minty Aeroes.

There were only cola bottles,
Joosters and milk bottles.

The only problem is my teeth
are rotting away!

Rebecca Holmes (9)
Golcar JI & N School

He Is . . .

He is taller than an elephant on another.
He is stronger than a sumo who is fat.
He is emptier than a bin that has never been used.
He is smellier than socks that everybody's smelly feet have been in.
He is uglier than a monster with scabs on.
He is fatter than a rugby player that's fatter than a sumo.
He is stupider than a baby, and . . .
He is smaller than an ant that's been run over and flattened
                                        and squashed.

Adam Clayton (8)
Golcar JI & N School

LAST IN THE QUEUE

When they gave out the sweets,
I was last in the queue.
There were no Mars bars or Milky Ways,
Starburst or Strawberry laces,
Twix or Twists,
Liquorice or lollies,
Chocolates or caramel.
Marshmallows or mints,
Double Decker or Dimes.
Tootie fruities or jelly beans.
There were only sherbet lemons and sherbet sticks.
The trouble is I don't like sherbet.

Emily Lockwood (8)
Golcar JI & N School

LAST IN THE QUEUE

When they gave out the sweets
I was last in the queue.
There were no mints or Maltesers,
Skittles or Smarties,
Mars bars or Milky Ways,
Twix or Twirls,
Crunchie or Caramel,
Picnic or Lion bars,
Dimes or Double Deckers,
Liquorice or Dolly Mixtures,
Jelly babies or Joosters.
There was only white chocolate,
The trouble is I'm allergic to white chocolate.

Daniel Hinchliffe (9)
Golcar JI & N School

LAST IN THE QUEUE

When they gave out the cakes,
I was last in the queue.
There were no apple cake or birthday cake,
Cheesecake or dolly mixture cake,
Elsy Cake or Frosties cake,
Ginger cake or hot cross buns,
Ice cream cake or Jaffa cake,
KitKat cake or nugget cake,
Orange cake or picnic cake.

There was only veg, veg and even more veg,
The trouble is I hate *veg!*

Charlotte Wadsworth (8)
Golcar JI & N School

LAST IN THE QUEUE

When they gave out the sweets
I was last in the queue.
There were no Rolos or Rocky bars,
Skittles or Sherbet lemons,
Cherry lips or Chewits,
M & M's or Mars bars,
Bubblegum or Bountys,
Twix or Twirl,
Red laces or Revels.
There was only liquorice,
The trouble is I am allergic to it!

Elizabeth Kirkby (8)
Golcar JI & N School

SCHOOLZ OUT FM

U feelin' down?
Got a bit of a frown?
Well call in,
And we'll put your frown in the bin!

We will play a tune
That will certainly go *boom!*
We are so cool
When there's no school!

Laura Taylor (10)
Golcar JI & N School

WHAT IS A . . . CHRISTMAS TREE?

A soldier guarding the presents stares.
Silently, listening
Waiting.
Silver circular buttons.
His torch steadily flickers through
motionless dark.

Eric Martin (9)
Lepton CE JI & N School

WHAT IS A CHRISTMAS TREE?

A soldier in parade guarding, watching
Every present carefully, staring without stopping
The stockings beside his legs getting ready for Christmas.

Tim Becker (9)
Lepton CE JI & N School

AUTUMN

Lovely and crunchy like a rosy red apple.
Scrunchy leaves, rough is the bark.
Beautifully the leaves flutter off the trees.
Rich colours, red gleaming and flame orange bright yellow,
                                    and shimmering green.
Green comes all the way with the evergreen.
   I love autumn!

Natasha Freeman (9)
Lepton CE JI & N School

AUTUMN POEM

In autumn they are shiny yellow and gold.
I love autumn because the leaves are lovely.
They are rusty and smooth.
I like the colours.
The one I like best is gold and yellow.
They all fall off trees when it is very windy.
They dance down from the trees.

Jordann Brooke (8)
Lepton CE JI & N School

AUTUMN

The rich rustic autumn leaves the colour of a burning flame.
Crunch, crunch like stiff cardboard dropping in a hard metal tin.
Crackle like the sound of a gigantic candle flickering.
A crispy light feather falling.

Chloe Jones (9)
Lepton CE JI & N School

AUTUMN POEM

Shimmering golden lemon leaves twirling down from the top of
the trees.
Russet coloured leaves crunched up to make a whispering sound.
Whispers of the leaves rustling when you jump in them.
Pretty rainbow-coloured leaves falling off the giant trees.
Leaves dance down to the ground.

Rebecca Ellis (8)
Lepton CE JI & N School

AUTUMN POEM

Rusty red leaves sounds like howling owls
The leaves twirling from trees.
The wind blows off the crunchy golden leaves,
Burgundy clattering crunchy rustling leaves.
Silver thick leaves,
They *crunch* and *munch* when you stand on them.

Lydia Mills (9)
Lepton CE JI & N School

A CHRISTMAS TREE

A soldier guards the presents.
His wide eyes winking slowly,
Steadily.
His green coat glistens with metals
In the lamplight.

Richard Asensio (10)
Lepton CE JI & N School

WHAT IS A ... CHRISTMAS TREE?

A pantomime woman acting silly.
Shining.
Twinkling as people admire her looks.
Her beads and buttons stand out dramatically.
Her pineapple coloured hair finishes it off.
Her beady eyes fixed on the audience.
Bells ring of the greatness.

Sophie Hirst (9)
Lepton CE JI & N School

WHAT IS A CHRISTMAS TREE?

Still in the corner,
Guarding your presents
Waits a big green soldier
Standing tall
Winking
Sparkling, spinning medals hang on his big green coat.

Lauren Bryden (9)
Lepton CE JI & N School

WHAT IS ... A CHRISTMAS TREE?

The green witch waiting for the children to come
To open their presents hidden beneath her cloak.
Silent still she waits.
With her wand at the ready she smiles to herself.
... Selfishly.

Helen Francis (10)
Lepton CE JI & N School

THE CLOCK

It stares out of its plastic framework,
It steadily lifts its stiff arms,
And tries desperately to smile.
Its heart beats slowly in time with its hands,
It waves as it sees its good friend the timer,
Its day passes with it having a staring contest,
It plays it with the timer and the TV.
It tells time without fail,
It travels forwards in time when appointed,
And travels back again in autumn.
Finally the contest finishes yet again,
Its batteries are flat.

Alex Pacynko (11)
Lepton CE JI & N School

THE CHRISTMAS TREE IS . . .

By the door
Waiting and winking
The soldier stands.

Guarding the presents
Waiting and winking
Heavy with decorations.

For the expected visitor
Waiting and winking
Not the slightest sound stops his work.

Waiting and winking
. . . Staring.

Samantha Pacynko (9)
Lepton CE JI & N School

THE BIKE

It is laid on the drive asleep, dreaming,
The ground is its only companion,
He did have friends once but now they're all dead,
He fears it is his turn to go to the skip,
His body is scratched and his shoes are worn,
The soft rubber on his handles is torn,
He knows that later that day he will be ridden,
And then locked out in the rain, neglected again,
But he never got the chance because then he closed his eyes,
And was taken away to die in the skip.

Laura Sykes (11)
Lepton CE JI & N School

WHAT IS . . . A CHRISTMAS TREE?

A green soldier
Standing smartly,
Guarding the shiny treasure.
His uniform decorated
With gold medals and stripes.

Danielle Boustead (9)
Lepton CE JI & N School

WHAT IS A CHRISTMAS TREE?

A half open green banana standing like a soldier,
Waiting for Santa to come.
Looking in every direction.
Look! Shining, gleaming and dazzling.

Lianne Todd (9)
Lepton CE JI & N School

AUTUMN POEM

Leaves twist off branches,
They twist and fall onto the ground.
You stand on them and they will crunch loudly.
You feel like Christmas is coming very early in the year.
Leaves are different colours each time of the year.
Leaves feel smooth, rough and rusty.

Leanne Midgley (8)
Lepton CE JI & N School

THE COMPUTER

He moans as his face is pressed,
But as he heals, he lights up for his master.
Then opening his mouth the disc goes in
And he sings as he chews it up.
Then spits it out when it is time to turn off.
When it is, he goes to sleep until the next time.

Vincent Armitage (10)
Lepton CE JI & N School

BABY

Loud screamer,
Sleepy dreamer,
Milk feeder,
Messy eater,
Nappy changer,
Noise maker,
Food lover,
Loves Mother.

Ashleigh Haigh (10)
Lepton CE JI & N School

AUTUMN POEM

Golden shiny leaves twist off trees.
Zooming to the floor.
Trees swivel side to side.
Branches snap off the prickly tree.
Leaves falling off the lovely smooth tree slowly.
They twirl all the way down.
The trees whistle and the branches clatter.

Miles Turner (8)
Lepton CE JI & N School

A PIANO

Music maker
Key presser
Space taker
Music holder
Heavy weigher
Note player
Joy creator
Money maker.

Bernard Martin (11)
Lepton CE JI & N School

AUTUMN POEM

Lemon leaves falling off the trees,
Rusty leaves falling on the ground.
Russet green falling from the dark blue sky.
I walked on a bunch of leaves and it went *crunch.*

I saw a zig zag leaf.
I felt a leaf and it felt smooth.
I ripped a leaf and it sounded like a sword.
I saw a leaf and its colour was light blue.

Liam Whittaker (8)
Lepton CE JI & N School

AN AUTUMN POEM

It's rough and strong.
There are plants everywhere around it.
Leaves flat upon the wall,
The leaves are brown, yellow, red and orange.
The trees can be dark brown or light brown.
Plants and nettles surround it and grass too.
Under the ground the roots spread around.
Big trees, middle trees, and short trees you can get.
Branches shake and break.
Some trees have leaves to make it look pretty.

Naomi Rank (9)
Lepton CE JI & N School

AUTUMN

Gold shiny leaves slowly drift off of trees.
Red leaves too,
Brown spiky twigs too.
They sound like *ooooooooohhhhhhhhhh.*
Like a whisper,
Beautiful sound,
And people love to jump in them.

Kerby McKenna (9)
Lepton CE JI & N School

LIZARD

Silent leaper
Small peeper
Colour changer
Rainforest ranger
Super senser
Bug cruncher
Quiet creeper
Nasty screecher.

Thomas Marsh (11)
Lepton CE JI & N School

HAMSTER

Short liver
Veggie eater
Animal lover
Great explorer
Messy cleaner
Ball traveller
Long faller
Water drinker.

Keith Hudson (10)
Lepton CE JI & N School

SUMMER HAIKU

The sun glows above,
Everyone is at the beach,
Swimming in the sea!

Alissa Smith (10)
Lepton CE JI & N School

THE SHARK

Ferocious murderer,
Deadly killer,
Twenty footer,
Heavy eater,
Ambitious endurer,
Sleek glider,
Blood scenter,
Lethal hunter.

Robert Coles (11)
Lepton CE JI & N School

BORDER COLLIE

Sheep chaser
Food waster
Great snoozer
Bad loser
Ball rounder
Angry farmer
Getting calmer.

Emily Durie (11)
Lepton CE JI & N School

WHAT IS . . . A CHRISTMAS TREE

A hedgehog in body armour ready to battle with his spears.
A soldier guarding the angel and her presents.
Standing tall armed with needles poking anything that
Tries to open them before Christmas morning.

Joseph Littlewood (9)
Lepton CE JI & N School

AUTUMN

Blue sky reddy orange leaves floating down to leafy floor, covered
in crispy leaves and twigs.
The lovely tree patterns on beautiful leaves.
Big snappy twigs falling down with the strong wind.
Splat! Wet and soggy leaves splatting on small heads!
Children standing on other dry crispy leaves making them crunch
like bones.
People rubbing their hands against smooth long white sticks
and small twigs.

Lucas Garg-Herrero (8)
Lepton CE JI & N School

THE MAGIC MOUNTAIN

On my mountain

There is an avalanche falling as quietly as a butterfly's flutter
Along with volcanic lava as hot as a blazing fire.

There is a river as cold as the Atlantic Ocean,
And as rough as a grizzly bear.

On my mountain

There is an eagle with a wingspan as
Large as an aeroplane.
And a monkey swinging from tree to tree
like an acrobat.

On my mountain

It is wild and happy, free and luscious.
And that is what is on my mountain!

Tom Hague (9)
Roberttown JI CE (C) School

WITCHES

Witches are horrible things;
They put a spell on fairies' wings!
They turn you into frogs;
And do cruel things to dogs.

Witches are so cruel;
They always break the human rule.

Witches are horrible things;
They put a spell on fairies' wings.
At night when it's really dark;
They do a spell with a hot spark!

Witches are so cruel;
They always break the human rule.

Georgia Trevitt (8)
Roberttown JI CE (C) School

THE WITCH WHO LIVES NEARBY

She lives in a haunted house,
Her cauldron is in the corner of her closet.

Nobody dares go near her because she smells of rotten fish.
Now everyone wears a sweaty gas mask
For you can smell her a mile away.

She has a big stuffy nose, with an enormous wart on the top,
Like a cherry on top of tasty white icing.

Everyone mocks the witch who lives nearby!

Jack Baldwin (7)
Roberttown JI CE (C) School

SWEETS!

Yum-yum yummy sweets,
Are the best of all the treats!

Sticky, slimy, sickly sweets;
Are the best of all the treats!
Lollipops to lick;
Always makes me very sick.

Yum-yum, yummy sweets
Are the best of all the treats!

Bubblegum is a mess;
Liquorice sticks are the best.
All these sweets give me bellyache;
I hope my mum doesn't make me a milkshake!

Melissa Wallis (8)
Roberttown JI CE (C) School

COLOUR

Red is the colour of leaves
Yellow is the colour of toys
Green is the colour of grass
White is the colour of boys
Black is the colour of hair
Brown is the colour of girls
Blue is the colour of the sea
Pink is the colour of clothes
White is the colour of pearls.

Emma Bolt (8)
Roberttown JI CE (C) School

THE BEAST

The evil dragon skims the treetops looking for his dinner,
curling his lashing tail.
Ready to erupt and breathe a flame of ice and snow.
He carefully sharpens his long talons and shines his metallic scales.
At night the beast then flies from his lair,
rippling his staggered spine,
and hissing his red tongue.
A knight spots the dragon, and throws a mighty spear,
only to find it slip off blue slippy scales.
It hisses and throws a mighty roar, and blows a flare of ice,
freezing the castle on which stood the knight.
Once almost home he gives a tremendous grunt and flies through the
mouth of the cave, into the teeth of stalagmites.
Now in the gloom he settles down to rest,
never to wake again.

Joshua Glassett (8)
Roberttown JI CE (C) School

FOREST SHADOW

Diamond summer,
Rose like white skin.
Shadow shine,
Mother Nature.

Flood beneath the ground,
Forest moon overhead
Death will be there
Love will not produce mist
Beauty leaves without a lie.

Ellen-Alyssa Gambles (8)
Roberttown JI CE (C) School

THE OWL IN A TREE

The owl's eyes are as big as the spread out sky
With the moon for the pupils.
The tree it lives in curves, as tightly wound as a coil,
In the night the hairy owl seeks its prey to find it's not a predator.

So watch out the owl is about.
Next time it takes a jump it might come down on . . .
        You!

Ellen Bellfield (8)
Roberttown JI CE (C) School

THE DRAGON

The cold yellow eyes as the dragon awakes.
In the mine of the mouth it heats up as it starts another morning.
A scale peeks out as it hears the roar of the master.
The scraping of the talons on the wall sharpening them.
Flapping wings as it goes out terrorising the towns.
Its eyes glare as it sees a knight trying to beat him once more.
The immense beast, can you see it or is it just a dream?

Samuel Bull (9)
Roberttown JI CE (C) School

LOVE IS . . .

Love is a friend you have forever,
Love is something we should treasure,
Love is a seed that needs to be planted,
Love is something we take for granted.

Love is something that keeps people together,
Love is a smile whatever the weather,
Love is something that grows like our hair,
Love is something we should always share.

Kerry Busby (10)
Roberttown JI CE (C) School

THE HANGING SPIDER

The spider is moving its web slowly like a slug running in a race.
The spider is waiting like a lion watching and waiting for its prey,
The branches of the tree stick to its silky web like paper stuck to glue,
He hangs there, protected by leaves as the rain tumbles down,
The web glistens in the moonlight,
He survived the night!

David Hall (9)
Roberttown JI CE (C) School

A DRAGON

He stands at the mouth of his cave
As still as the air breeze
Burning a forest that seemed to look like a crisp wasteland
Bit by bit it turned to ashes
With a swish of his tail he could perish an army
With a stamp of his heavy body he would cause an earthquake
Which helps mankind to fade away into the mid air
Where the stars are sparkling like silky silver.

James Ross (8)
Roberttown JI CE (C) School

UNHAPPY GIRL

Chorus
Crying in the sun,
Crying in the moon,
Crying in the evening,
Crying all day long.

Weeping in the corner,
Sighing in the sun,
'What will happen next?' I said,
Now tell me, I'm being bullied.

Chorus

Turn around the corner
A thump in the mouth,
I go into a shelter,
Now tell me I'm being bullied.

Chorus

The bully comes along,
A fight for a fight,
Scared at the sight
Now tell me I'm being bullied.

Chorus

A friend comes along!
A surprise for me,
I'm not used to this,
Now tell me, am I going to be bullied?

Chorus 2

Laughing in the sun,
Laughing in the moon,
Laughing in the evening,
Laughing all day long.

A transformation appeared on me,
A lesson about bullies,
Now I know how to deal with bullies
Now tell me, no one gets bullied.

Chorus 2.

Hannah Pickering (8)
Roberttown JI CE (C) School

THE DAY I MET A DINOSAUR

The day I met a dinosaur
It had three legs.
Its name was Tryhorn
And it had sharp teeth.
I bowed to the humongous monster
And she curtsied back.
As she licked her lips she said to me
'Do you know I'm a meat eater?'
My face went pale.
I spluttered '*What*!'
'Yes, it is a surprise
But I don't eat people with too much hair.'
So I went to the river
To catch her some fish.
She said to me
'No need to bother, I'm okay.'
I was compassionate to the dinosaur
Of course she did share her love with me.
It was nearly time for her to go home
With a swish of her tail and a mouth full of laughter
I was gone.

Charlotte Glaves (7)
Roberttown JI CE (C) School

THERE'S A SPIDER IN MY BED

There's a spider in my bed
And I can't get to sleep
It crawls up my leg
I can't help but peep.

There's a spider in my bed
He wants me to stroke him
But he knows I won't
I've tried to touch it
But then I think *No Don't!*

There's a spider in my bed
And actually it's quite nice
So when my head is tingling
It eats the head lice!

Samuel Crossley (8)
Roberttown JI CE (C) School

SPECIAL SURPRISE

Your eyes are as blue as the crystal sea,
You run like a cheetah sprinting to catch its prey.
You're the spices rumbling in my tummy.
You're the fizz of my shandy being gulped.
You're the aeroplane that carried me to Australia
And the excitement I have had with you.
I think of you when I buy baggy jeans
Because you have them too.

That is why you're my best friend.
    Alastair.

Gavin Harrison (9)
Roberttown JI CE (C) School

CHILDREN

Children play all night and all day,
Mischievous and cheeky in the middle of May.
Sweets and chocolates they nibble all the time.
They drink fizzy pop like lemonade and lime.
Dirt and worms are liked by boys,
But girls are different and love cuddly toys.

They always watch telly and play computer games,
Some are bullies and call people names.
Deep down they are sweet angels waiting to be found.
They're always begging their mum and dad for a little more
than a pound

But overall they're wonderful, they can even run a mile,
They always play and have a great day and do nothing else but . . .
Smile!

Kellie-Jo Jeffery (8)
Roberttown JI CE (C) School

THE RISE FROM THE DEAD BOX!

The hinges are racked
The demons will rise.
The hamastsaurus will kill,
The hinges are made out of a dinosaur's soul.
It shudders as you enter with a dark, gold, solid, *key!*
The aliens will charge to the top of the crater . . .
I smell the lava of the demon's breath.

Be endangered!

Luke Hardy (8)
Roberttown JI CE (C) School

BEWARE THE VENOMOUS BOX

Beware the venomous box

In this box lives the dead
The ripe red blood falls with a ghostly screech
When you open this box skeletons, ghosts,
The headless horseman
Give you a *trick or treat*
I hear ghost cries, *woooo*
Dinosaur's vicious bites
Living pumpkins
A man with a dagger stuck in his heart
A horse with one eye
Another ghostly cry
And an eye with a pencil stuck through
Beware the venomous box
My box looks like
It's made of bones and eyes
On every bottom corner bloodstains on each bone
Cobwebs all over.

Beware the venomous box.

Bethany Stead (8)
Roberttown JI CE (C) School

WINTER

The snow is white and crispy,
and if you get up early
you will hear the robins sing.
In the street you will hear the people sing.
In the church you will hear the choir sing.
In the town you will hear the band play.

Alexandra Auty (8)
Roberttown JI CE (C) School

THE SPIDER AND THE WEB

The sleek, velvety mesh is woven by a
strong spider that never gives up.
Night falls and it's lunchtime for the spider as it hunts
Secretly for its prey.
Suddenly the fly flies into the web and
the spider catches the helpless fly
in the deadly still sickly web of
multiplying mystery blood throttling mesh.
Day time dew on the web of disturbance
and of
puzzles of mystic mystery.
The web is now dismal and
the fly now dies a most
painful death.
As it has been wrapped up in
sticky wet silk.
The sleek mesh gets all ruined
holes and no middle
where the middle must be.

Kirsty Crowther (8)
Roberttown JI CE (C) School

KETCHUP

You're as black as a chocolate cake,
Your eyes are like sparkling spheres
Glowing in the moonlight.
You're as soft as my tracksuit bottoms,
You're the colour of coca cola.
You make me laugh when you roll over on my legs.
You're the best cat in the whole wide world.

Matthew Stone (8)
Roberttown JI CE (C) School

UNHAPPY GIRL

She was hunched up on a chair
With her arms folded,
A frown on her face,
No one to speak to at all.

The bullies pointing and laughing,
A tear fell and the drip dropped.

She was sitting near the fountain
Nothing to play.
All playing in a group,
Not caring for her.

The bullies all laughing and pointing,
A tear fell and the drip dropped.

She was fiddling with her hair,
The space around her grew and grew,
She knew she had no friend and never would.

The bullies all pointing and laughing,
A tear fell and the drip dropped.

Kirsty Gee (8)
Roberttown JI CE (C) School

MY MUM

Your skin is as velvet as a skirt.
You are a rose in the sunset.
You are a bedroom with me at night.
You are as happy as a joke.
You're like a dress covering my body.
Your voice is beautiful as a song.

Laylaa Whittaker (8)
Roberttown JI CE (C) School

THE MAGIC BOX
(Based on 'Magic Box' by Kit Wright)

I will put in my box . . .
a door that leads to space,
a pearl from an oyster shell,
a silver shooting star that does not shoot.

I will put in my box . . .
the howl of a wolf,
the roar of a hungry lion,
a fire breathing donkey
and a flying rat.

I will put in my box . . .
a cloud that tastes like candyfloss,
and a coconut tree that grows hazelnuts,
a tooth made out of gold.

My box looks like . . .
crystal water glittering in the sunlight,
a heart cut out of the top to let the wishes in,
the sides are a glistening ruby red.

That is what I shall put in my box!

Georgina Barry (8)
Roberttown JI CE (C) School

MY MUM

She is a rose to me red and velvety when I touch her.
Chocolate is her dream, tea in bed too.
Velvet by the side of her bed, she feels it at night.
She is a star to me always there for me.
She is the best.

Joanna Clarkson (8)
Roberttown JI CE (C) School

THE MAGIC BOX
(Based on 'Magic Box' by Kit Wright)

Open my box and see . . .

Spooky dreams and wonderful nightmares,
Ice cube in a hot frying pan never melting,
Buzzy bee in the air falling asleep making slurping noises.

In my box there is . . .

A cold sun,
And a warm avalanche,
See a blue frog and
A green horse.

Look at my box and see . . .
gold and silver spiral hinges with a red top,
rainbow coloured sides but don't forget
the stamps on the side of yellow chickens.

Robert Ives (9)
Roberttown JI CE (C) School

DOWN IN THE CORNER OF THE CUPBOARD

Down in the corner of the cupboard, there's a rat,
Down in the corner of the cupboard, there's a bat.

Down in the corner of the cupboard, there's a wizard,
Down in the corner of the cupboard, there's a lizard.

I only went to get my ball, but nobody told me about the
faaaaaaaaaaaaaaaaaaaaaaaaall!

Matthew Miller (7)
Roberttown JI CE (C) School

MY CAT FLOSSY

A ball of fluffy fur
A cute little purr
Awoken with a start
A softly beating heart
Soon you are at play
But sleep during the day
Then into the world you explore
Through the open door
You wash yourself clean
Where have you been?
Then when you are fed
You curl up on my bed.

Daniel Mott (7)
Roberttown JI CE (C) School

SUN POEM

The sun is a golden orange
Hung on pale blue string.

Its beaming light
Shines so bright
Upon my sunglasses.

As it gets darker
the sun goes down
so it becomes
Sunset!

Laura Baldwin (10)
Roberttown JI CE (C) School

HANNAH

You're a new baby dolphin
flipping in the sea.

Your skin is as soft
as silk.

You're as blue
as a blue jumper.

You're as runny
as a chunk of melted chocolate.

You make me laugh
when I'm feeling down.

You're like a
red rosy tulip.

You support me
when I've been bullied.

You're the Coke
fizzing in my belly.

You're like the
leather on my sofa.

You're my favourite person
you make me

Smile.

Sara-Jayne Pollard (9)
Roberttown JI CE (C) School

THE ENCHANTED BOX

In my box there's . . .
The smallest dinosaur,
And the biggest mouse,
The warmest ice cube,
And the coldest lava.

In my box there's . . .
The loudest squeak of a mouse,
And the softest pound of a drum.

In my box there's . . .
The smoothest sandpaper
And the roughest cottonwool.

In my box there's . . .
Perfume that smells like manure,
And chocolate that smells like mud.

In my box there's . . .
Cabbage that smells like sand
And carrots that taste like pencil lead.

In my box there's . . .
Black rain and green sky.

In my box there's . . .
Bins with arms,
And walking tables.

In my box there's . . .
Sad faces,
And happy faces.

My box is . . .
Marble with a gold lid
And silver jewels with spiral corners.

James Booth (9)
Roberttown JI CE (C) School

SUNSET

I am a blinding golden sun.
I shimmer over the calm delicate shore,
as the breeze drifts by.

I spread brightness
across the crystal sky.
I blaze out my glimmering beam
over the burnished sea.

I am as round as the magnificent Earth.
I am the lustrous sun which spreads
happiness all over the world.

Bethany Ruston (9)
Roberttown JI CE (C) School

FOOTBALL

Kick the ball,
Score a goal
Watch out!
Don't fall!

Use your skills
With the ball
Pass it quick
As you call!

Try to win
For your team
1-0
That's brill!

Elliot Binns (7)
Roberttown JI CE (C) School

THE MOON

The moon is all glistening
It shines with the stars,
Spaceships see it
When flying to Mars!

The moon is so bright
It could give you a fright!
But it will always come
And wish you good night!

The moon has some friends
His best is the sun,
Together they'll spend hours
Having some fun!

The moon is spectacular
Better than the Earth,
Scientists think it's magic
I wonder how much it's worth?

The moon is the best
I think it's ace,
But it will always
Stay up in space!

Abigail Binns (9)
Roberttown JI CE (C) School

THE SUNSET

The blazing sunset watches over the continents.
The majestic sun reflects on the gentle sea.
It shines like a golden medallion.
It's a bright orange.

Matthew Sumner (8)
Roberttown JI CE (C) School

SHOP TILL YOU DROP!

From the far end of the car park,
Dashing through the rain,
Automatic doors open,
Inside,
Escalators,
Heaving with people,
Some leaving,
Others arriving,
Hold tight to Mum's hand,
Don't want to get lost.

From shop to shop
'Can we go for something to eat?'
'Soon,' says Mum.
Into another shop,
Then another.
'Can we go for something to eat?'
'Soon,' says Mum.
Into another shop
Then another.
'Now can we go for something to eat?'
'Alright then.' She says.

Upstairs in the food court,
More people,
More queues.
Finally getting served,
Looking around,
'Empty table!'
'Where?'
'Over there.'

We sit down,
Dump shopping bags on the floor,
And begin to eat.

'We don't have to go anywhere else do we?'

Hannah Mather (8)
Roberttown JI CE (C) School

CRYING GIRL

Crying girl sitting in the corner
Crying all day long!
Shivering in the frost
She has been bullied
By somebody.
No one to play with,
No one to talk to.
She scurried around
The wide playground
To catch her attention.
A gang of boys stand
Around her in a circle.
She wishes she was brave enough
To walk through them.
They say nasty things
About her.
Who wants to play with her?

She stands in the shadow cold
and alone,
Nothing to do, nothing to say,
Crying in the classroom
Crying in the cloakroom.

Amy Peacock (8)
Roberttown JI CE (C) School

SEASONS

Four special seasons throughout the year,
Some full of sadness, some full of cheer,
But this poem's all about your opinion,
So many reasons, maybe one million.

To start off the verse, it has to be spring,
Jolly and bright, can't upset just a thing.
A chorus of birds tweeting amongst the silence,
Anything can be better than horrific violence.

Winter's the next, nearly full of mist,
Like a freezing cold icicle gently being kissed.
Scarves and gloves; we all need protection,
From the blistery cold, not all perfection.

Picturesque and golden, can you guess?
Autumn of course at its best.
The whispering of the wind that howls by,
Each different colour of autumn may never die.

'Save the best till last' as they say,
Summer is my favourite is that okay?
Children playing in the glorious sun,
Humid heat, but lots of fun.

Four special seasons throughout the year,
Some full of sadness, some full of cheer.
But that poem's all about your opinion,
So many reasons, maybe one million.

Olivia Jeffery (10)
Roberttown JI CE (C) School

CAMELOT

Hath seen all in glory
All rivers flowing through,
So many appointed enter,
But no one unappointed enters Camelot.

Although have so many come out,
But little hath gone in,
All never did come back
To everlasting Camelot.

Although hath no one seen,
All king in all crown jewels,
All they see is through nights
That will never end
On living in Camelot.

But those will be cursed
And only the brave will be uncursed
Upon reaching Camelot.

Along they go all flattered and stunned
To see such glory
That they shall go such a way,
To see the great Camelot.

All have reached who have to come
But oh! Such a pity
That a weak strengthless girl
Was cursed
By great and powerful Camelot.

George Edmond (10)
Roberttown JI CE (C) School

MY DOG

My dog is great,
He's really cute!
But the problem is
He ruined my mum's best suit
But I still love him.

He's really sweet,
Soft and furry,
We give him a treat,
His hair all curly,
But I still love him.

He lays down on the carpet begging for food
My mum says '*No*!'
And gets in a mood
And so I go
But I still love him.

Lexy Clavin (9)
Roberttown JI CE (C) School

MUM

You're a tulip that's purple and you never die,
You're like donuts watering in my mouth,
You're like a silk coat,
You're good at cuddles that makes me proud,
You make me feel like S Club 7 are here every day.
When I eat my donuts I think of you.
When I drink hot chocolate I think of you.
When I go to Blackpool you're there,
And that's why you're my favourite person.

Bethany Robinson (9)
Roberttown JI CE (C) School

THE LARKIN'S DOG

A poor old woman had a dog,
It was always barkin',
It's name was Buster of course,
And the woman's surname was Larkin.

She sniffed and coughed all day long,
And said the wind was nipping,
And when the dog got in the way
She gave it a good whipping.

Her husband shuffled in and out,
He wasn't very supple,
They weren't at all what you might call
A really pleasant couple!

Christopher Thomas (10)
Roberttown JI CE (C) School

FRIENDSHIP

F   riends are kind and caring
R   elated, it feels we are.
I   n and out we run about,
E   very day we play,
N   othing will stop our friendship
D   isaster!
S   ometimes we fall out
H   elp! We are
I   mportant
P   eople!
    Friends are cool!

Jessica Mott (10)
Roberttown JI CE (C) School

SUMMER DAY
AND THUNDERY NIGHT

The people say
It's a wonderful day
The sun is up
But the sky is grey.
The thunder is back again
But a lot of people are in pain.
It's a sunny day
So humans can play.
It is raining on the Earth
But a baby, he's just been given birth
So look up in the sky
You might see a beautiful bird
I wonder why?

Jacob Sheriff (9)
Roberttown JI CE (C) School

IT

It creeps through the jungle with the slightest of ease
Even the smallest have to get on their knees
For it creeps so low and stalks at night
It hides in its cave when it gets light
It takes down the mightiest predators, the cheetahs, the lions,
the tigers too
It can do somethings nobody can do
And in the middle of the night it . . .

Roars!

James Sutcliffe (10)
Roberttown JI CE (C) School

RACING

Driver climbs into his seat
Engine starting, feel the heat
Racing on the racing track
There's no time for going back.

Ripples of heat, forming waves
Now they're racing through the caves
Going out the other end
Time to go right round the bend.

Now he's on the final straight
History will soon be made
Nearly there, his speed is up
Over the line, he's won the cup!

Simon Gray (9)
Roberttown JI CE (C) School

I'M FRIGHTENED OF A TREE

You're the spook of the night
You get out at the night and fight
Your bedtime is one o'clock
You've never been scared
You're mean to be a bean
You're the venomous tree of the night
You know what to do at night
Your branches make me scream
You're like a man at night
It is the shadow of a tree
That I am frightened of.

Robinson Wade (8)
Roberttown JI CE (C) School

A Beggar And A Thief

Holly is on a diet,
Since she's been to the vets
They put her on the weighing scales
To see how much she weighed.
The results were overwhelming
I could just not believe how much the
Scales passed the weight she should have been.

We started her on a diet
No nibbles snacks or treats,
Even when she's sitting pretty
I'm not allowed to feed.

My dogs become a beggar
And if I'm not careful a thief
Anything that's edible
She definitely now will eat.

Holly is on a diet because it's healthy to be thin
She needed to be on a diet
Because she looked like a wheelie bin.

Now she's started to look thin
She's stopped all her begging
And I'm sure she will now feel better
Now she's toned and trim.

Holly is my bestest friend
And I'm determined to keep her thin
Because I want to keep her
Today.
Tomorrow and next week!

Keeping healthy is the best thing you can do!
I've seen what happened to my dog
And it could easily happen to you.

The conclusion to this poem
Is don't ever over eat
You could become like Holly
Overweight
A beggar and a thief.

Aimie Crodden (10)
Roberttown JI CE (C) School

PEACE AND CARE WITH UNICEF

P　eace. Children need peace.
E　ducation. They need that to learn
A　buse. No none of that
C　are. They need mums and dads
E　lectricity instead of candles.

A　comforting home
N　o war
D　octors for medication

C　lean clothes to wear
A　fun life
R　ight, right
E　veryday's best.

W　ater. Clean water
I　nto a play time. Lots of toys.
T　ransport to get places
H　ave a good day at their house now.

　　　　. . . *Unicef*

Alasdair Hurst (9)
Roberttown JI CE (C) School

CHOCOLATE!

Chocolate is the best of treats;
Better than normal sweets.
Caramel and dairy milk;
Makes me feel of warm silk.

Chocolate here and chocolate there;
Chocolate seems to be everywhere!

Chocolate is the best of treats;
Better than normal sweets.
Galaxy and Mars bars;
Make me feel of glittering stars.

Chocolate here and chocolate there;
Chocolate seems to be everywhere!

Abigail Wallis (9)
Roberttown JI CE (C) School

IF I WAS AN ANIMAL

If I was a monkey, I'd be the best at swinging
If I was a lion, I'd be bad at singing
If I was a hippo, I'd be splashing in mud
If I was a cheetah, I'd be running as fast as I could.

If I was a giraffe, I'd be as tall as the trees
If I was an eagle, I'd glide on the breeze
If I was a hedgehog, I'd not cross the road
If I was a shrew, I'd not want to meet a toad.
*If I was a human I'd be as
happy as can be.*

Thomas Dixon (10)
Roberttown JI CE (C) School

LIFE ON MARS

Mars is a deserted place
There are aliens on Mars
It is in the middle of space
They looked like space.

Life on Mars, life on Mars
I wouldn't like
A life on Mars.

This planet is dark red
When the sun goes round the Earth
The aliens go to bed
And a new planet is at birth.

Life on Mars, life on Mars
I wouldn't like
A life on Mars.

Kate-Arline Miller (10)
Roberttown JI CE (C) School

LOVE IS . . .

Love is something you should always treasure,
Love is a friend you will have forever,
Love is a seed that needs to grow,
Love is something you need to show.
Love is something you need to share,
Love is something you should never tear,
Love is something that keeps you together,
Love is a smile whatever the weather.

Siobhan Brogden (10)
Roberttown JI CE (C) School

IF I RULED THE WORLD

If I ruled the world
there would be no wars
and no chores.

If I ruled the world
there would be no heartache
but only love.

If I ruled the world
there would be no poverty
but only riches.

If I ruled the world
everyone would smile and
no one would cry.

If I ruled the world
it would be the best place ever!

Shelby Hutchison (9)
Roberttown JI CE (C) School

THE SUN!

The sun is like a fresh golden daisy,
The sun is like a disco ball in the sky,
The sun is like a beautiful gold butterfly,
The sun is like a giant pie.

The sun is like a huge fireball,
The sun is like the tiny grains of sand,
The sun is like a gold beachball,
Covering the lakes and the land.

Natasha Riches (9)
Roberttown JI CE (C) School

WINTER POEM

Winter snow lays frothed on the ground,
Snowflakes running all around.

Iced up grass,
Is what crackles when you pass.

Winter snow lays frothed on the ground,
Snowflakes running all around.

Soft morning and night snow,
Lays thick on the ground for all to show.

Winter snow lays frothed on the ground,
Snowflakes all running around.

Gradually but soon snowmen appear
But when summer comes they disappear.
Winter comes again, they reappear.

Winter snow lays frothed on the ground,
Snowflakes running all around.

Maria Nawaz (11)
Roberttown JI CE (C) School

PEACE

P   eace no more gun tanks or ships to go off to war that's what I want.
E   ntertainment like swings and parks to play in that's what I want.
A   ntidote and needles for medicine for when we are ill, waterbottles
    and beds that's all I want.
C   lothes, clean clothes, lots of clothes, a washer to wash them in
    that's all I want.
E   ducation pens, books, boards, desks, chairs and a school to put them
    in, that's what I want.

Richard Brown (9)
Roberttown JI CE (C) School

RADISH

You are my
woolly feeling
that never ends.

You're the
chocolate melting
in my mouth.

You're the
sadness melting
in my heart.

You're my hoody
keeping me as
warm as you are.

You're singing
year 3000
to me.

You are the golden
sun shining
down on me.

You're the
Tango fizzing in my
mouth.

You are
the time
I'm a good boy.

Alastair McDonald (8)
Roberttown JI CE (C) School

IF I OWNED CHOCOLATE

If I owned chocolate I would eat, eat, eat.
If I owned chocolate I would keep, keep, keep.
If I owned chocolate I would throw, throw up,
If I didn't own chocolate I would cry, cry, cry.

If I owned chocolate I would scoff, scoff, scoff.
If I owned chocolate I would show off, off, off.
If I owned chocolate I would be happy, happy, happy.
If I didn't own chocolate, I would cry, cry, cry.

Kerry Brooks (9)
Roberttown JI CE (C) School

COAL

Rough as a cave,
Shiny as diamonds,
Black as jet,
Cold as ice,
Lots of layers.
It smells of dust.
It has been pushed.
Thousands of years old.
Hidden underground.
Smooth on some bits.
Smells of the sea.
Heavy as brick.
Looks like a cliff.
Has loads of cracks.
When lit the coal has life.
It is as warm as lava, it is rainbow colours.
It comes to life with its spirit.
It ends up as old, grey ash.

Martin Tucker (8)
St Joseph's RC Primary School, Huddersfield

COAL

Black as jet
Sparkling like gems
Rough and bumpy
The coal has little tiles on it.
It smells like old earth.
Coal is made from trees and earth squashed together in layers.
The miners dug it from underground.
Long ago children toiled to bring it out.
Dirty hands, dirty faces,
Light your fire, keep you warm.
See the colourful flames revealing the coal's secret
Watch the embers glow
Soon there will be nothing left
But cold white ash.

Rachel Lamont (8)
St Joseph's RC Primary School, Huddersfield

THE HAPPY NEW YEAR DRAGON

He lives in a sunny place,
His face is such a disgrace,
His breath smells like mud,
Deep down inside he is really good.
Look at those scales red, pink and gold,
Shame on him because he looks really old.
Jumping up and down like he hasn't a care,
But hey what's this?
Fireworks in the air!
While everyone shouts
Happy New Year!

Kayleigh Paxman (8)
St Joseph's RC Primary School, Huddersfield

WINTER

See winter race through the woods
See the streams shivering away,
Slide on the iced rivers,
Stamp on the crunchy leaves.
See the icicles stabbing into your back
Play snowball fights.
See bare trees with their black fingers twitching away
Up above the grey clouds are sprinkling rain from the sky.
My teeth chatter away like a cold crunchy leaf.
See hedgehogs hibernate in their cosy warm dens.
See the foxes searching for food
Now you have watched winter
Spread its icy carpet over the land.

Jessica Finn (8)
St Joseph's RC Primary School, Huddersfield

MY THOUGHTS

I lie in bed with my covers over me
reading my horror book.
I hear screaming and the clock ticking.
It strikes twelve and there's footsteps
creeping up the stairs, a creak in the floorboards
and a shadow on my wall.
There's tapping on my window and
banging on my door,
I think I'm getting scared, so I'll read a little more.
I'm shivering in my bed squeezing tight
to my teddy bear.
I jump out of bed and run into my mum's room,
she calms me down.

Shauni Macken (8)
St Joseph's RC Primary School, Huddersfield

MY THOUGHTS

After I've read my horror book,
I scurry up the stairs
I hide myself under the covers
But,
I'm not afraid, not me.

I can see a vampire's shadow
They've come to get me
So I cuddle up to my teddy,
But,
I'm not afraid, not me.

The clock strikes twelve,
The witching hour
Bats are flying above me
But,
I'm not afraid, not me.

At last I peep out of my covers
And the ghouls are gone
Mum screams
But,
Yes I am afraid, yes me!

Sophie Detraux (8)
St Joseph's RC Primary School, Huddersfield

AUTUMN

Autumn is when the leaves dance around in the air.
Autumn is when the spiky conkers come off the trees.
Autumn is when the animals hibernate.
Autumn is when the leaves fall like a swan's feathers falling.
Autumn is when the frost appears on the trees.

Shannon Fleming (8)
St Joseph's RC Primary School, Huddersfield

GREEN

Green is the colour of leaves that float in the air.
Green is the caterpillar that turns into a butterfly.
Green are the trees growing apples.
Green are the patterns on a beautiful butterfly.
Green is the grass swaying in the wind.
Green is the crayon we use.
Green is the paint on the bars around school.

Jason Batters (8)
St Joseph's RC Primary School, Huddersfield

YELLOW

Yellow is the colour of sweet lemon so sour
Yellow is the colour of daffodils swaying in the sunlight
Yellow is the sun shining on a summer's day
Yellow is grain ripening in the field
Yellow is the colour of sweetcorn - yum!
Yellow is the colour of a sunflower growing so high.

Jolene Wike (9)
St Joseph's RC Primary School, Huddersfield

MY DRAGON

In China dragons
Swirl and twirl,
Dance and flutter,
All around the town
Like your dreams
Come true.

Bret Barraclough (8)
St Joseph's RC Primary School, Huddersfield

WINTERTIME

Take a cold frosty morning,
with twinkling snowflakes fluttering
from the snowy sky.
Icicles hanging from the tip of the roof.
Snow dancing in the cold air,
And children throwing snowballs at each other
and making snowmen.

Add some snowballs flying through the air.
Snowflakes fluttering from the grey sky,
And Jack Frost dancing across the fields.

Mix in the bare black trees which stand alone
in the cold winter air.
Some children ice skating on the frozen panel.

Blend it all together and there you have it
        Winter.

Antonia Casson (8)
St Joseph's RC Primary School, Huddersfield

MY DREAMTIME BOX

My dreamtime box is full of . . .
The twinkling of the stars.
The heat of the sun.
The lazing of the flowers.
The blue of the sky.
The sand of the deserts.
The growing of the plants.
The animals playing.
The gleaming of the moon.
The singing of the birds.

Lucy Calvert (8)
St Joseph's RC Primary School, Huddersfield

A WITCH'S BREW

Tail of a puppy dog,
Bark of a log.
An eye of a blue newt,
Half a jar of jute.
The horn of a unicorn,
A jar full of frog spawn.
A hair of a rhino,
A tooth of a dino.
A bolt of lightning,
The fin of a greenling.
Mix it together and you have a witch's
Brew straight from the cauldron.

Jacob John (10)
St Joseph's RC Primary School, Huddersfield

ROLLER COASTERS

In and out, round and round
underground
hear that sound screaming voices
rumbling stomachs
loop-the-loop, do not puke.

Going slow, calming down
next thing you know
going back round
finally you stop a sigh of relief
when you get off you weigh a heap.

Shaun Finn (10)
St Joseph's RC Primary School, Huddersfield

SCHOOL DINNERS

Monday's dinner looked a treat
A plate of crawling nits.

Tuesday's lunch I didn't eat
The plate was glued with bits.

Wednesday's dinner looked like pie
That had been cooked in soap.

Thursday's lunch was an old school tie
And two strands of stale rope.

Friday's dinner was gungy goo
And a welly filled with meat.

It's Saturday now and I've got the flu
Plus I'm too weak to eat.

Stephen Gandy (10)
St Joseph's RC Primary School, Huddersfield

WINTER

Snow is falling from the sky
Children sledging in the snow
Bare trees with silver icicles hanging
From the branches
Children's lips turn blue
Whilst they build a snowman in the snow.

Silly boys are skidding on the ice
Ice skaters skating on the frozen ponds.
Parents chatter and shiver in freezing snow.
Winter is here, lots of fun and time to play.

Lauren Breslin (8)
St Joseph's RC Primary School, Huddersfield

COLOURS OF THE WORLD!

Blue is the bright sky,
Red is runny blood,
Yellow is the hot sun,
Brown is a tasty orange,
Pink is small mouse ears,
Green is the tall grass,
Black is a rain cloud,
Grey is a lazy donkey,
Amber is a traffic light,
Purple is your parents' old disco pants,
Gold is a prize medal,
Bronze is a rusty metal fence,
Multicoloured is the world!

Tanya Allert (10)
St Joseph's RC Primary School, Huddersfield

PINK

My favourite pop star is Pink
I'd write it in permanent ink
When she sings she is so loud
If it was me I'd be so proud
I love her hair she changes a lot
She even changes it when she's on the trot
I'd like my hair like that
But my mum said I will have to wear a hat
Some day I want to be like Pink
And wrote in permanent ink.

Charlotte Cosgrove (10)
St Joseph's RC Primary School, Huddersfield

MY...

My cat acts like a rat,
My rabbit has a bad habit,
My guinea pig is as small as a twig.

My candle is bigger than a handle,
My sweets are treats,
My drink is the colour of pink.

My teddy is called Eddy,
My pencil is smaller than a stencil,
My rubber is as green as flubber.

Candice Slee (10)
St Joseph's RC Primary School, Huddersfield

GOLD

Gold is the colour of sheet scaly wings,
Gold is the colour of a well earned trophy,
Gold is the colour of a crown on a king's royal head.
Gold is the colour of wheat drying in the sun,
Gold is the colour of a necklace on a neck,
Gold is the colour of autumn leaves drifting down to the ground.

Ben Wilson (8)
St Joseph's RC Primary School, Huddersfield

COAL

The coal is black as a dark cave.
Darker than a cat.
Darker than a witch's cloak.
Black as jet.
Rough as a cave wall.

It glitters in the light
When you light it.
All the flames flutter around.
Then it turns into ashes.

Oliver Thompson (8)
St Joseph's RC Primary School, Huddersfield

SEASONS

Spring is flowers growing tall,
And baby lambs being born.
Summer is sunbathing at the beach,
Swimming in paddling pools all day long.
Autumn is leaves fluttering
from the trees,
and people wrapping up nice and warm.
Winter is playing snowball fights,
Robins sitting in the snow.

Amber McNulty (10)
St Joseph's RC Primary School, Huddersfield

GREEN

Green is great, it's like grass
Green is the colour of leaves
Green is a caterpillar crawling munching away.

Green is a sour apple, Mum puts in a pie
Green is the colour of jealousy
Green is the colour of seaweed.

Green is great!

Joseph Gillespie (8)
St Joseph's RC Primary School, Huddersfield

SEASONS

Winter arrives with the shivers
Wrap up nice and warm
The snow is white and crisp
But still gives me the shivers.

Springing into sunshine
Come the little lambs.
Skipping through the daffodils
Bringing joy to you and me.

Summer brightens up the day
As school closes down
Playing out and having fun
On beaches, parks and in pools.

Autumn comes as colourful leaves fall down
Running through them in the park
Listening to the rustle and *crunch*
As we kick them all around.

Shona Peel (10)
St Joseph's RC Primary School, Huddersfield

MAGICAL COLOURS

White is the wonderful snow falling everywhere
Black is the night sky cast over the world
Red is the school jumper representing St Joseph's
Blue is the wavy seas swishing and swaying all over the place
Yellow is the blazing sun lighting the world
Green is the grass in your garden
Silver is the night sky filled with stars.

What wonderful colours they all are.

Joshua Whittaker (10)
St Joseph's RC Primary School, Huddersfield

COLOURS

Blue is the clear sky glinting in the air
Yellow is a candle glowing in your bedroom
Green is a piece of holly with bright red berries
Black is the newspaper headlines
Orange is Jupiter flowing in the sky
White is the snow falling on the playground
Red is our school bookbag waiting in the classroom
Pink is a little pig running around on the soft grass
Brown is the Christmas pudding with custard over the top
Grey is a cloud casting the sky
Gold is a gold star to be proud of
Silver is a mirror to look at yourself, oh you look
            lovely!

Jacqueline Wike (10)
St Joseph's RC Primary School, Huddersfield

JACK

There was a boy called Jack
Who owned a big cat
He lived in a house
And was scared as a mouse.

Jack was cleaning his room
With a big wooden broom
When he was done
He went down and got a bun.

Jack was watching TV
And it showed a picture of a deep blue sea
After he went to the park
And saw his good friend Mark.

Joshua McDermott (10)
St Joseph's RC Primary School, Huddersfield

THE MAGICAL DREAM

When I'm laying in my bed
thoughts are spinning round my head.
I cannot sleep, what shall I do?
I'll go to sleep and have dreams too.
And in a blink I fall asleep.
Mum's at the door having a peep.

I dream a beautiful unicorn
prancing with his golden horn,
how wonderful to live in this magical place
where fun and laughter is on every face.
Oh how I wish I could be
with my galloping beauty by the sea.

His diamond mane flows in the breeze
makes you think of swaying trees.
He cannot stop, his heart beats fast
I wish this dream could always last.
I really love this horse you see
I wish I could take him home with me.

If he can't live for evermore
my heart will be so very sore.
As my friend was being born
I dreamt he trotted on the lawn.
He jumped the fence at a frantic pace
I'll love him for ever, my friend called Ace.

Siobhan O'Toole (10)
St Joseph's RC Primary School, Huddersfield

COAL

Coal is as black as jet.
It's sparkly as silver.
Rough as a cave wall.
Coal smells like old metal.
Coal was made thousands of years ago
From all the twigs and trees.
They all got squashed and changed.
When coal is lit it blazes into colour
Like yellow, orange and red.

Luke Chadwick (8)
St Joseph's RC Primary School, Huddersfield

COAL

Black as jet
It has a slight sheen to it
Smells like a piece of earth, cold as ice
Bumpy and rough as a witch's nose
Formed years and years ago deep underground
Deep underground hands and knees have been cut
Inside a secret of its life is waiting to be revealed.

Gillian Harris (8)
St Joseph's RC Primary School, Huddersfield

AUTUMN

Leaves flutter beautifully.
Conkers drop madly.
Squirrels leap gymnastically.
Bonfires crackle loudly.
Autumn is fun!

Jodie Turnbull (8)
Seacroft Grange Primary School

MY DOG

M y dog is called Jazz,
Y ellow eyes that look like flies,

D own to the sand to jump,
O ut to the playground,
G o and run about.

Robert Hodgson (7)
Seacroft Grange Primary School

MY DOG

M y dog is called Tigger,
Y ellow eyes growing bigger.

D igging holes in the ground.
O r hiding bones in the flower bed.
G oes and runs around the shed.

Mayte Carrington (7)
Seacroft Grange Primary School

MY DOG

M y dog's name is Trigger,
Y ellow eyes that grow bigger.

D og yaps at the postman
O r digs in the garden
G rowls at passing people.

Nathan Hall (7)
Seacroft Grange Primary School

HARRY POTTER

He swishes his mauve shabby wand,
As he curses words upon the world.
His cloak thrashes against the midnight sky
While the magic cascades.
The scar of that saved himself
While sacrificing a mother.
The unknown secret of being not a full human
But a wizard!

Tamara Atieno (10)
Seacroft Grange Primary School

AUTUMN COLOURS

Cold wind blowing
Red leaves spinning
Brown leaves tipping
Orange leaves curving
Yellow leaves rolling,
Black leaves curling,
Rustic leaves stumbling.

Abeygayle Spink (8)
Seacroft Grange Primary School

DAZZLING DOLPHIN

A dolphin looks like a steel bullet gliding through a cerulean sky.
Its silver silky skin, a shimmering sparkle in the water.
Dolphins disappear in a flash, then click back in a second.
Their bedazzling bodies glisten in the beautiful sunlight.

Bethany Dickinson (9)
Seacroft Grange Primary School

THE WIND

The wind whistles through the night.
It is cold,
Cold as ice.

When is it going to *stop?*
The wind is wrapping round me
Freezing me to the ground.

The wind crashes into my face.
And pulls me back into a tree.
Banging my head I feel sick.
And I feel poorly
I am going to be sick.
I am going home now.
To get into bed.
Twirling, whirling,
I am blown home to bed.

Jason Iddison (9)
Seacroft Grange Primary School

THE SEA

The sea is a rampaging rhino
Thundering to the shore
Beating on the soft sand
Ramming into innocent people
on the beach.

When he leaves and gets back to his hideout,
It is calm once again.
The beach becomes a bustling sunlit fantasy.
The people leap about not knowing
That the rampaging rhino is still down there.

Matthew Haigh (9)
Seacroft Grange Primary School

RAINBOWS

Rainbows have hundreds of colours.
Any you can think of?
Any you can see?

Golden, yellow, dazzling.
Red and sparkling silver.

Rainbows make you happy
In every sort of way.
Lovely shining rainbows that
Dazzle through the day.

Blue and shining, velvet,
Silky orange and rosy pink.

Rainbows have hundreds of colours.
Any you can think of?
Any you can see?

Gemma Matthews (10)
Seacroft Grange Primary School

THE TIGER OF THE SEA

The sea is like a tiger.

When the storm comes it will lash his razor
teeth upon his prey.

But when the storm disappears he will
return to his lair.

After, when he leaves the beach
it is all calm.

But the silence will not last.

Jonathan Turpin (8)
Seacroft Grange Primary School

WINTER COLOURS

White frost
Makes the grass hard and spiky.

White icicles
Slippery and cold.

Blue sky
Bright and beautiful.

Blue lips
Cold and dry.

Red fingers
Ready to drop off.

Red sunset
Melts you.

Black shadows
Scary and dark.

Black slush
In gutters.

Silver stars
Twinkling like jewels.

Silver moon
Shimmering brightly.

Winter is here.

Dominic Lynch (8)
Seacroft Grange Primary School

WINTER COLOURS

White icicles
hanging like daggers.

White snowflakes
swirling in the breeze.

Blue lips
sore and dry.

Blue sky
with frosted clouds.

Red sun
rising joyfully.

Red fire
blazing warm.

Black ice
slippy all over.

Black slush
in the gutters.

Silver moonbeams
shimmering beautifully.

Silver stars
dazzling like diamonds.

Winter is here!

Demi-Jo Monica Powell (9)
Seacroft Grange Primary School

SWEATY TRAINERS

Andrew's got some trainers
Smelly, sweaty trainers
Stinky, dirty trainers
He loves them very much.

Purple, pink, pongy trainers,
Toe logo flashing through the night.
Mum yells 'Take them off!'
Our Andy hides them away.
Mum hunts them down with her Supersonic smeller.
Puts on gloves and a mask,
And wangs them down the cellar.

Our Andy's got no trainers,
No smelly, sweaty trainers
No pink and pongy trainers,
They're down the council tip.

Rebbecca Bulmer (10)
Seacroft Grange Primary School

SUZIE

Suzie was my pride and joy,
Her ebony eye would stare,
Her overweight ginger body,
Carefully under my care.
But when she passed away,
The night of my concert,
I sang for her,
Even though times were incongruent.
But now I know.
She's not coming back,
And memories are all I have.

Ezra Tren-Humphries (10)
Seacroft Grange Primary School

MINOTAUR

Screaming scaring all through the night.
You cannot sleep in case he gives you a fright.

The horns on his head.
The sharp teeth in gum.
The hair on his back is so shiny and sleek.
His legs are strong.
His arms tearing into people
I wonder when it will be my turn?
Theseus came, the noise suddenly stopped.
We started the noise then,
We cheered and cheered our hero.
He came out of the dark hole
Dragging the terrifying monster,
Still terrifying even when dead.
Silent now, its hairy arms
Flopping and swaying side to side.
Gladness took over.

Jodie Matthews (10)
Seacroft Grange Primary School

FAT EDDIE

Fat Eddie is so handsome,
I love him so much,
His hair is soft and silky,
His locks I love to touch,
His teeth are long and yellow,
At his athletic form, I stare.
I'm sure you'd feel the same as me,
You see, Fat Eddie is my hamster.

Sarah Robinson (10)
Seacroft Grange Primary School

AUTUMN

Golden leaves floating down.
Red leaves fluttering down.
Brown leaves swirling down.
Orange leaves twirling down.

Strong wind howling.
Gentle wind murmuring.
Light wind whispering.
Wild wind screeching.

Squirrels scamper for food.
Birds fly far away.
Hedgehogs run for cover,
Wasps sting and die . . .

Richard Burgess (9)
Seacroft Grange Primary School

FREEZING!

The sky is blue and grey.
It's cold, it's freezing!

Animals are freezing!
They need help.

Can you hear their voice?

You must help them.
They need food,
They need shelter,
They need water.

Then they will love you.

Adam Vollans (7)
Seacroft Grange Primary School

THE VICIOUS VIPER

The vicious viper slashes the moonlight trees.
Then there is a vinewhipping breeze,
He waits in a moaning, muttering rage,
Then he points his venomous tail ready to launch again.

He hisses like an old man.
Then he starts to get mad.
And then he rattles like a can.
He groans and moans.
And then he starts to get weakened.
Then he grumbles 'I'll be back another day.'

Matt Parker (11)
Seacroft Grange Primary School

THE SILKY DOLPHIN

Splash!

The silky dolphin leapt out of the
crystal clear, cobalt sea.

The sparkling, silky dolphin bounded
over the glamorous, translucent waves.

The dolphin laughed with lots of cheer.

And all the other dolphins heard and came
to see what was happening.

The laughter came from the silky dolphin's
family.

Jade Entwistle (8)
Seacroft Grange Primary School

THE WIND

The wind is like an enraged eagle
Swooping down to Earth, as it gathers energy
To make a monstrous whirlwind.

As the twister hits Earth it devours
nearly everything.

It sucks up millions of houses.

The clouds are like voluminous ebony pillows.

As the storm reduces

It leaves devastation in its wake.
Fractured fences, crumbled houses and -
The horrible cries that were left behind.

Ashley Thomas (8)
Seacroft Grange Primary School

SNOW

It is snowy.
Throw a snowball or build a snowman.
White houses,
White fields,
White hair,
White clouds,
White cars,
White windows,
White trees,
White ice,
White snow.
I like going out in the snow.

Lee Slatcher (7)
Seacroft Grange Primary School

SNOWFLAKE FALLING

White snow.
Snowflake falling
Blue sky.
A snowman outside.

Let's go out and have a snowball fight.
I am cold.
I am going inside.
I am still wrapped up.

I am not cold.
I am warm.
I am near the fire.
Snowman cannot melt because it is cold.

Let's go outside.
Let's go shopping.
We will walk and throw snowballs at Mum.
Mum will be mad!

Callum Parker (7)
Seacroft Grange Primary School

THE RAIN

The rain is like a cascading fall of gem drops.
Falling from the grim, grey, midday sky.
And then the sadness stopped
The wind picked up,
The sun went down
We were in total darkness.

Ryan Schofield (11)
Seacroft Grange Primary School

THE MOON

The moon is like a shimmering eye
in the midnight sky.

The moon is a diamond shining in
the dark clouds.

The moon is a silver ball, reflecting
on the hot, flaming, yellow sand.

The moon is a round circle shining
brightly in the velvet blue sky.

Danielle Grosvenor (9)
Seacroft Grange Primary School

MY DOG

M   y dog is called Gizz Mo,
Y   oung and weak,

D   rinking in the garden
O   r hiding his bones,
G   rowling for more.

Cassie Carrington (8)
Seacroft Grange Primary School

MY DOG

M   y dog is called Jabba,
Y   et he is black, big and dangerous.

D   oes he run around the play area
O   n his own?
G   oes and plays catch with me.

Kieran Cooper (8)
Seacroft Grange Primary School

RUSH RUSH

Monday morning time to get out of bed.
It's school today!
Time to go to the bathroom.
But sis is in the bath.
Hurry I'm really busy, busy.
I'm going to be late.
Oh hurry up.
It's school today!
So come out of the bath!
Brush, brush my teeth.
It's school today!
Time to change my clothes.
Put my coat on, put my shoes on.
I'm not late!

Ayisha Mistry (7)
Swinnow Primary School

MY HAPPY WEEK

Being happy is . . .
Sweets,
Holiday in Spain and Scarborough,
Playing football with Daniel and Liam,
Playing tig with Billy Boy,
Getting ready on time for school,
Play in the snow with Billy, Darren and Tommy,
Getting homework back on time,
I like playing chess with Daniel and Elliot,
Doing maths when I do it right,
I have a happy week.

Thomas Hart (7)
Swinnow Primary School

THE WRITER OF THIS POEM

(Based on 'The Writer of this Poem' by Roger McGough)

The writer of this poem . . .
Is as funny as a silly clown juggling some balls,
As strong as a large sumo wrestler having a fight,
As gentle as a fluttering butterfly flying above the sky.

As fast as a charging cheetah running through the wood,
As slow as a staggering old person crossing the road,
As happy as a super smiley face smiling away,
As silly as a crazy joke being told.

As worried as a timid mouse beneath the stairs,
As stationary as a still statue in the city,
As angry as a charging bull running around,
As brainy as a laptop computer's mind storing a file,

   I'm the writer of this poem, that's me!

Alistair Ryder (8)
Swinnow Primary School

CONVERSION CRAZY

The players are ready, ready for playing,
Out of tunnel they come.
The ref is blowing, blowing his whistle,
To say the game's began.
The players are scoring, scoring and winning,
This means a team has won.
The fans are happy, the players are famous.
So everyone's having fun.

Connor Rutherford (9)
Swinnow Primary School

THE WRITER OF THIS POEM
(Based on 'The Writer of this Poem' by Roger McGough)

The writer of this poem . . .
Is as beautiful as the twinkling stars,
As strong as an orange crane,
As gentle as a grey nibbling mouse.

As fast as a running football player,
As slow as my teacher writes on the big board,
As happy as the shining sunshine,
As silly as wobbling jelly on a plate.

As grumpy as Mr Taylor, a school teacher,
As smart as a clicking calculator,
As cheeky as the Cheeky Girls,
As sly as a black thief at night.

The writer of this poem is me!

Georgina Ford (9)
Swinnow Primary School

MY LIFE IN SOUTH AFRICA

I lived in South Africa with loads of sunshine.
The flowers bloom up in loads of little lines.
Animals jump in large groups to keep together
for safety of one another.
There are pools all over to get away from heat
and boy what a stress relief.
The days are hot as an oven
and the nights are cold as a freezer.

Cheyenne Shan (11)
Swinnow Primary School

THE WRITER OF THIS POEM
(Based on 'The Writer of this Poem' by Roger McGough)

The writer of this poem . . .
Is as handsome as the birds and the bees,
As strong as a sneaky stranger,
As gentle as the dazzling moonlight.

As fast as a fighting football player,
As slow as a slippy slimy slug,
As happy as my school teacher,
As silly as a jelly on a plate.

As intelligent as an encyclopaedia,
As dangerous as a dancing devil,
As naughty as a sly fox,
As smelly as a disgusting oil tank,

   The writer of this poem is me!

Oliver Colling (8)
Swinnow Primary School

A POEM ABOUT ME

I am the youngest in the house
I roar like a lion not a mouse
I have got green eyes
My hair is brown
Because it makes me happy
I don't like being cross
It makes me sad.

Darren Henderson (7)
Swinnow Primary School

116

THE WRITER OF THIS POEM
(Based on 'The Writer of this Poem' by Roger McGough)

The writer of this poem is a bold lad,
As strong as the undertaker,
As gentle as skin on a poodle dog.

As fast as a football player,
As slow as a cat.
As happy as someone on their birthday,
As cheeky as my brother,
As silly as a grumpy lion.

As sweet as Mrs Chidsey,
As angry as my dad,
As crazy as my sister.

David Todd (9)
Swinnow Primary School

FORMULA ONE POEM

F   ormula One is the best
O   ne track is different from all the rest
R   alf Schumacher is Michael Schumacher's brother
M   ichael is the best
U   s watch as they go round and round
L   ast lap go for chase
A   ll pit lanes are busy changing fuel.

O   n the track they fastly go
N   ow on the track they barely know
E   very driver is a different international.

Thomas Royston (9)
Swinnow Primary School

THE WRITER OF THIS POEM
(Based on 'The Writer of this Poem' by Roger McGough)

The writer of this poem . . .
Is as slim as a green grasshopper,
As strong as a fat elephant,
As gentle as the sparkling snow.

As fast as a charging rhino,
As slow as a slimy snail,
As happy as my school teacher,
As silly as a funny joke box.

As small as a little mouse,
As clumsy as a silly clown,
As colourful as a beautiful butterfly,
As brainy as a headteacher.

    The writer of this poem is me!

Tamra Morton (8)
Swinnow Primary School

YEAR SIX

Y ear six is my last class here,
E very day we're getting closer to high school,
A fter half term SATs are looming,
R eady and waiting, working hard.

S etting high standards to achieve,
I want to achieve
X cited but sad, as Swinnow I leave.

Chelsea Belk (10)
Swinnow Primary School

GRIFFINS ARE MAGNIFICENT

Griffins are magnificent,
Griffins are so innocent,
Griffins have such fiery pride
Griffins have a lion's hide.
Griffins roar up to the sky,
Griffins fly so very high.
Griffins are so magical,
Griffins are quite mythical.
Griffins have such beauty.
Griffins hunt while owls are hooting.
Griffins' feathers falling red as fire.
Griffins fly past an angel playing a lyre.
Griffins went up past the clouds.
Griffins just fly all around.
Griffins are so very proud of their poem
Griffins!

Rowena Walmsley (10)
Swinnow Primary School

ENGLAND

E   very four years in the World Cup.
N   ever win it.
G   oal! Owen scores.
L   eeds Robbie Fowler makes it two.
A   lan Smith gets a red.
N   igel Martin lets one in.
D   anny Mills swears at the ref.

James Geldard (10)
Swinnow Primary School

MY FAMILY AND FRIENDS

M y family all started in 1991
Y ou gave me a life when I needed to start

F riends and family watched me growing up
A fter all I still am your child
M y world changed when I started to grow
I n all becoming a young little girl
L ittle still I change I'm growing every day
Y our heart is filled with proudness with all the things I do

A nswers to questions that you told me
N othing has changed since I've grown older
D ifferent people know me in different ways

F amily have passed away, but I still miss them
R idiculous arguments have gone on in the past
I n the end we've got through
E every day we're getting stronger
N ot knowing that I'm still here and I'm never going to leave
D oing things that I know were wrong
S till I have my family.

Rebekah Cardy-Warren (11)
Swinnow Primary School

MY LUV, MY BRUV!

One day a strange thing happened,
It popped into this world,
Two staring eyes just looked at me,
My shoulder then turned cold.

We took him home the next day,
He smelt fresh and brand new,
The adults fussed around him
Saying, 'Googie, googie goo.'

I didn't understand it,
Until I found the love,
What would I do without him,
My one and only *bruv!*

Megan Reilly (10)
Swinnow Primary School

MY MUM

When I popped into this world
my mum was there to see it.

When I said my first word
my mum was there to see it.

When I took my first step
my mum was there to see it.

When I first went to school
My mum was there to see it.

When I go to high school
My mum will be there to see it.

When I go to university
My mum will be there to see it.

When I get married
My mum will be there to see it.

When I have a baby
My mum will be there to see it.

When my mum grows old and goes
I will be there to see it.

Jodie Rutherford (11)
Swinnow Primary School

MY BROTHER

My brother means the world to me,
even though I do not see
I love him with all my heart,
to me he is the most important part.

I sometimes wish he wasn't there,
but really we're a perfect pair.
Sometimes he is really bad,
which makes me really mad.

We can play really well
until one of us goes to tell.
Bruv what would I do
if I didn't have you.

Jessica Teggart (10)
Swinnow Primary School

I AM SPECIAL

I   am special

A   nd there's nothing you can do about it.
M   onday morning going down the corridor.

S   omebody's got to be special every day.
P   eace and quiet that's the key.
E   ach and every one of us is special.
C   all on me when you need a hand.
I   f life's pretty hard, I'll understand.
A   lways come to me if you have a problem.
L   osing control is not the answer.

Craig Bell (11)
Swinnow Primary School

MY DREAM

When I am in bed I twist and turn,
into a magical world -
full of hopes and wishes.
I dream and dream.

My magical dream,
with all my wishes -
seems to be so real!

When I wake up,
I pause my dream -
I stare around my room -
the dream is suspended!

On my starry night sky,
I will sit beside a magic waterfall -
dreaming even more!
My dreams a wonder, my dreams a star!

Laura Riley (10)
Swinnow Primary School

KEITH

He is a red sofa always angry
He's a bear always cross
Keith's a park jumping about
He's a fuzzy cat running everywhere
He is a tongue always moving
He's my big brother.

Helen Bennett (9)
Swinnow Primary School

POEM ABOUT ME

My name is Jason.
I have big blue eyes.
My hair is short and spiky.
My teeth are white and bright.
And my feet are big too.
They might stand on you.

Jason Firth (7)
Swinnow Primary School

RABBIT

R   ushing rabbits fast and nimble
A   lways hopping and leaping
B   ouncing bundles of fluff
B   roccoli is a favourite
I   n her hutch she munches and crunches
T   ill it is dusk and then we cover her up.

Jade Lee (9)
Swinnow Primary School

SNOWFLAKES

When the snow falls you think it's great,
When you play in the snow with your mate,
When you go home you are late.

When you wake up the next grey, cloudy day,
It's snowing again your parents say,
You can go out to play.

Laura Griffin (9)
Thorpe Primary School

MY TEACHER

My teacher is lovely,
My teacher is kind
My teacher is special.

My teacher shouts sometimes,
But she doesn't like it
She'd rather have a laugh and talk about it.

She shouts if she has to but most
Of the time she talks.
My teacher cares about everyone
And she also cares about you.

My teacher is not big,
My teacher is not small
She is just the right size of them all.

My teacher is the best teacher *in the world!*

Abigail Fleming (11)
Thorpe Primary School

WHEN THE RAIN DROPS

Raindrops falling off rooftops.
Everyone says it will stop.
The rain does not stop it just goes plop, plop, plop.

The rain goes splash, splash, splash,
The thunder goes crash, crash, crash,
The lightning goes flash, flash, flash.

Jodie Handley (8)
Thorpe Primary School

Mums!

Mums are special
Mums are true
Mums will always stand by you!

Mums help you out all year through
Paper, scissors and some glue
Making models, painting pictures too!

Cooking, cleaning, loving you
When you're poorly, when you're sad
She'll make you better, she'll make you glad!

They might not always be there
But they will always
          Care!

Sarah Hall (10)
Thorpe Primary School

Sunny Day

Kids are playing in the sun,
We are having lots of fun,
I'm enjoying a chocolate bun.

Birds are flying in the sky,
My joy is rising way up high,
What I'd give to fly, fly, fly.

Abbiegale Baylis (8)
Thorpe Primary School

MY FRIENDS

M y friends are so cool
Y ou sometimes meet them at school.

B est friends are trusted and very special
E mma at home who's a best friend and
S arah is funny also
T anya from football.

F rances is a pal and
R achel and Kim are too
I need Vicky as well as
E mma being my best friend. A
N ever-ending friendship
D on't forget this message
S tay friends forever!

Charlotte Sturrs (10)
Thorpe Primary School

LISTEN TO THE RAIN

As I sit here listening to the rain
I can hear water falling down our drain.

I hear raindrops
Dripping on the rooftops.

All the noises I can hear.
The clouds are over, the sky's not clear.

James Armitage (10)
Thorpe Primary School

LOVE

I will love you till . . .
We grow old and have grey hairs,
Until I say the last words,
And die of old age,
And be buried, in a grave.

If I still love you,
I will light a candle in the dark,
And celebrate our love,
And leave the candle to burn and burn.

I want to give you,
Any wish you want,
Your favourite flavour that will never go away,
The love of me for ever,
Just about anything you want.

I love you more than,
The brightest star in the sky,
The love of my mum and dad,
The day I go on holiday,
The first ride in a car.

Hannah Eatwell (11)
Thorpe Primary School

HULLABALOO

Hullabaloo
Is better than you
And every line
Doesn't have to rhyme.

Hullabaloo
Is really fun
It's much better
Than an everlasting bun.

Hullabaloo
Is so, so fun
It's much, much better
That's it I'm done.

Jordan Braithwaite (10)
Thorpe Primary School

NEVER ENDING UNTIDINESS

I got lost in my bedroom once
Lost in a corner just like a dunce,
Socks and shoes and toe nail bits
Lots of dark holes down the pits!

Lost in my bedroom what shall I do?
I could clean it but what could my mum do?
She would probably pass out then have a fit
Then fall down into a pit!

I'd leave her there for about a week
Then I'd take a little peek,
She would see me looking down the pit
Then she'd give me a great big hit!

She would shout and she'd yell
The more she did the more I'd rebel
I screamed and I shouted
The more I did then more she doubted.

So even now I'm still there
Eating a really mouldy pear,
So take my advice *clean your room*
Don't just stand there *get a broom!*

Rachel Whitlam (11)
Thorpe Primary School

MY TEACHER

My teacher is caring
My teacher is sharing
My teacher is fair
She will always be there.

She is loving
She is kind
She is true
And is always there for you.

My teacher shouts
She will send you out
And where you're bad
It will make her sad.

So take my advice
And try to be nice.

Rebecca Jones (10)
Thorpe Primary School

MY BEST MATES!

My mate Emma she likes the weather!
My mate Rachel she's very grateful!
My mate Jodie she sucks dodeys!
My mate Charlotte she likes scarlet!
My mate Becky she hates being called specky!
My mate Lorna, her mate's Laura!
My mate Helen she likes melon!
My mate Vicky she's very picky!
And then there's me well I'm just . . .

Me!

Victoria Winn (11)
Thorpe Primary School

MY FAMILY

My mother is mad
she can't find her notepad.
My dad is happy
and sometimes snappy.
My sister's angry
because she's hungry.
My brother is in the army
and he goes barmy.
My brother is working
and always smirking.

Amy Hill (10)
Thorpe Primary School

BLUE IS

Blue is the sky
Blue are my eyes
Blue is beautiful
Blue is my car
Blue is my ball
Blue is a star
Blue is bluebell flowers
Blue is my bedroom
Blue is my pen
Blue is my book
Blue is my door
Blue is the sea.

Blue is my favourite colour.

Kyle Nicholson (8)
Withinfields Primary School

GARETH GATES

G areth Gates is really cute.
A nd I like his hairstyles.
R otten Will Young had to win,
E nding his tour was upsetting.
T rainers and jeans he likes to wear,
H is first album is really good.

G areth is the best.
A ll I do is think of you.
T he best song you have done is Suspicious Minds.
E veryone should like you.
S oon I will meet you face to face.

Louisa King (9)
Withinfields Primary School

WINTER POEM

W inter is cold
I n the icy roads
N aughty children peep at their presents
T ea is chicken on Christmas Eve
E ggs and
R ashers of bacon too.

I ce is cold and turns to water
C old ice is on the ground
E veryone is cold in the house.

Alexander Jones (7)
Withinfields Primary School

FAVOURITE THING

I like dogs
they're furry like teddy bears
with floppy ears just like me.

Pizzas round as a ball
cheese
just like the sunshine.

My friend is Natalie,
ginger hair just like ginger cake
bright colour like a rainbow.

I like rabbits they're sweet
as me they wiggle their nose
just like me.

Rebecca Robson (10)
Withinfields Primary School

JAMES

J   ames is lonely and poor,
A   peach is small and also *big!*
M agnificent peach and very juicy
E   lephants are big, James is small.
S   ponge is fat and Spike is thin.

P   eaches are juicy,
E   lephants have four legs, a centipede has a million
A   nd James has got lots of friends.
C   ats are nice, so is James
H amsters crawl not like James.

Sophie Broadley (9)
Withinfields Primary School

LITTLE CHILDREN

Ten little children were very fine,
One grabbed a vine,
Then they were nine.

Nine little children sitting on the gate,
One chased after Kate,
Then they were eight.

Eight little children living in Devon,
One went to Heaven
Then they were seven.

Seven little children sitting on some sticks.
One did some tricks
Then they were six.

Six little children in a beehive
One did a dive,
Then they were five.

Five little children sitting on the floor
One broke a door
Then they were four.

Four little children sitting in a tree
One ate his tea
Then they were three.

Three little children sitting in some glue,
One slipped in some goo
Then they were two.

Two little children having lots of fun
One was gone,
Then they were one.

One little child all alone
He was the hero
Then they were zero.

Danny Quirk (8)
Withinfields Primary School

WOOD POEM

Bird
peck, peck,
eat, tweet,
sparkling leaves
on the trees,
wolves howling
crying for food,
foxes hunting,
smelling meat,
woodpeckers
pecking on
the trees,
looking for
maggots in the
dark trees,
owls howling
magpies looking for gold,
Farmers moving
foxes away
from their home.

Elliot Kebbie (8)
Withinfields Primary School

THE HILL

On a silent and most calming night
In my house there was a brilliant sight
An owl woke me up
I went to the window.

I rubbed my eyes
And stared out of the window
I saw a hill
A beautiful hill.

And there I saw
An owl go through a door
Then the door shut
And then I saw
On the front of the door, an owl
There on the door, some writing
I smiled at the picture of the owl
And went back to bed.

Ashley Johnson (7)
Withinfields Primary School

FAVOURITE THINGS

F   rom the start, my favourite thing was
A   small toy duck,
V   ery, very small duck.
O   nce I was one year old, I had a fave book,
U   nder my mum's watching eye, I played. In
R   eception I loved the sand,
I   t was powdery yellow dust, that I loved so much,
T   hat I let it run out of my hand.
E   nergy was what I had lots of.

Sarah Jones (11)
Withinfields Primary School

THE RAINFOREST

I prowl slowly through the magical rainforest,
waiting for something to leap out from the sparkling,
indigo water . . .
     Splash
I run away from a tiger who's a *Man eater*
     Growl
A black panther caught in a trap. I leave him.
     Whine - whine
Small, cute, black and white panda cub
abandoned by its mother. I take him downstairs
out of my rainforest bedroom.

The panda I called treacle. (Hamster)
The panther, Percy (the black cat)
The tiger, Winnie (the orange and white cat).

Stephanie Cooper (11)
Withinfields Primary School

WORLD WAR

W alking to our trenches
O pen fire!
R unning to no-man's-land
L ying there, shot down.
D angerous tank near our base.

W arplanes fly and bomb
A ttacking enemy base
R acing through missions.

Harry Metcalfe (9)
Withinfields Primary School

WEEKDAYS AND THE WEEKEND

Monday is a fun day
Tuesday is a choosing day
Wednesday is a making friends day
Thursday is the worst day
Friday is a dry day
Saturday what is the matter day
Sunday is the done day.

Grace Metcalfe (7)
Withinfields Primary School

MY COOL DOG

My dog is so cute,
She likes a bit of fruit,
Her name is Tess,
And she makes a mess.
She would die for chicken,
and never stops lickin'
She loves to walk
but never talks.

James Eastwood (9)
Withinfields Primary School

MY DOG SANDY

S   o cuddly as a bear
A   nd has dark golden fur
N   aughty as a monkey
D   rinks after she's been on a long, long walk
Y   ou are giddy, playful and very happy.

Jade Markwell (9)
Withinfields Primary School

A Secret Wish

My secret wish is not to be told,
Is it a magic land hot or cold?
Nobody knows about this wish,
Is it to swim like a fish?
It's something good, I give you my word
Is it to fly like a bird?
To find my wish you have got to wish.

Amy Neill
Withinfields Primary School

Secrets

S ecrets you should never let them slip.
E verybody should keep them.
C onserve your secrets.
R etell your secrets to your friend.
E veryone should have a secret.
T rust your friends with your secrets.
S *hhhh.*

Lauren Abrahams (10)
Withinfields Primary School

My Room

My room is yellow and bright,
but dark and warm at night.
It has loads of toys,
and of course no boys.
My music in my room goes *boom*
I like it in my lovely room.

Kirsty Wade (9)
Withinfields Primary School

THE SHADOW

Shadows hide behind the people,
Ghostly shadows guard the steeple,
Shadows run carefully around,
Making not a single sound,
Shadows hide in cases,
Shadows hide in hidden places,
Shadows also hide down the alley,
While people wander and dilly-dally,
Shadows are just like stalkers,
Following unsuspected walkers,
Shadows take the shape of a thing,
They open their mouths but do not sing,
These faceless beings sneak about,
but we know they're there without a doubt.

Christopher Taylor (10)
Withinfields Primary School

MY CAT

My cat is extra cute and cuddly,
My cat is annoying sometimes,
My cat scratches me and bites me,
My cat is really smelly, most of the time,
My cat pops my balls and makes holes in my sofa,
My cat is always sleepy,
My cat plays when he is not sleeping,
My cat is a cry baby,
My cat is only ten months old,
My cat's name is Pepsi,
    I love my cat and he loves *me!*

Roxanne Woolridge (9)
Withinfields Primary School

DESERTS

The soft amber rich sand,
cactus in the middle.

The dark orange horizon sky,
with Arabian camels passing by.
The Arabian feel for an Arabian night,
bare and saggy sand dunes in the curry orange sky.

Camel to the oasis, gerbil rat to its hole,
rattle snake down the steeple, brrr it's ever so cold,
ever so scary,
and ever so darey.
I can hear a noise,
with all these hairy creatures!

Sophie Lesiak (10)
Withinfields Primary School

WHEN I WAS ELEVEN

When I was one I weighed a ton
When I was two I lost my shoe
When I was three I sat under a tree
When I was four I went to the store
When I was five I felt alive
When I was six I picked sticks
When I was seven I went to Devon
When I was eight I went out of the gate
When I was nine I was fine
When I was ten I got a hen
When I was eleven I flew to Heaven.

Laurence Wike (8)
Withinfields Primary School

UNDERWATER

Underwater is amazing
You'll see things you have never seen before
Look at that seaweed that looks like it's
Going to reach out and grab you.

There's a sparkly orange dish that shines like the sun.
A shiny yellow fish that floats like a jellyfish.
There is a huge grey whale that looks like a giant raincloud.
And a great white shark with blood spread around it.

Don't you think being underwater is amazing?

Katie Whittaker (11)
Withinfields Primary School

SNOW

Soft snow has fallen during the night
The grass snuggles under a carpet of white
We climb in our wellies and slide on our bellies
Then button up warm make footsteps in circles
Around the white lawn.

Jessica Alexander (8)
Withinfields Primary School

MY NUMBER POEM

When I was one I saw the sun
When I was two I lost my shoe
When I was three I hurt my knee
When I was four I crawled on the floor
When I was five I learnt to dive

When I was six I learnt some tricks
When I was seven I went to Heaven
When I was eight I opened a gate
When I was nine I drank some wine
When I was ten I used a pen.

Gareth Clayton (8)
Withinfields Primary School

THE MONSTER

I saw a monster,
A monster last night
He's not really scary
So he doesn't give me a fright.

He's brown and gooey
And he looks kind of gloopy.

The monster doesn't like the light.
So he stays up and looks at me in the night.
I saw a monster, a monster last night.

Jack Wade (8)
Withinfields Primary School

MY POEM

S   now
N   ew toys
O   pen spaces
W   inter
M   uffins
A   pple pie
N   ew year.

William Forsyth (7)
Withinfields Primary School

WHAT MY FRIENDS ARE LIKE THAT ARE COMING TO MY PARTY

Faye is funky, funny and friendly!

Abbi is amazing, adorable and absurd!

Leanne is loopy, lovely and luscious!

Dannielle is daring, dazzling and dangerous.

Katie is kind, keen and a karaoki queen!

Amy Triller (11)
Withinfields Primary School

CAT

M y cat runs round the house all night,
Y our cat is black and white.

C ats are always tired all day
A cat can be different colours
T he cat is house trained.

Dale Smith (7)
Withinfields Primary School

THE BALLOON

Balloons go high in the sky,
Balloons go pop when they drop,
Balloons are very light,
But still hold them tight,
Or the wind will carry them away.

Danielle Booth (10)
Withinfields Primary School

THE FOUR SEASONS

Winter is fun
winter is cold
you can go out
and play on your
sledge in it.
Snow is white
snow melts
snow is flaky
snow is small
dots you
can make a snowman
out of snow
summer is warm
summer melts
all the snow
in summer you
can play out more
summer's much
better than winter.
In summer you get to have barbecues.
Spring is nice because all the flowers come up
and birds start to sing and baby animals are born.
In autumn it's freezing
and in winter all the leaves turn brown
and fall off the trees.

Keoasha Kendall-Brown (8)
Withinfields Primary School